REFLECTIONS ON INEQUALITY

REFLECTIONS ON INEQUALITY

EDITED BY STANISLAV ANDRESKI

CROOM HELM LONDON

BARNES & NOBLE BOOKS NEW YORK
(a division of Harper & Row Publishers, Inc.)

First published 1975
© 1975 by Stanislav Andreski

Croom Helm Ltd. 2-10 St. John's Road, London SW11

ISBN: 0-85664-245-2

Published in the USA 1975 by
Harper & Row Publishers Inc.
Barnes & Noble Import Division

ISBN: 0-06-490179-3

Printed in Great Britain by
Redwood Burn, Trowbridge and Esher

CONTENTS

	Introduction	1
1	Revolution and the Class Structure **Aristotle**	9
2	On Inequality and Corruption **Niccolò Machiavelli**	16
3	Class Struggles in Florence **Niccolò Machiavelli**	19
4	Class and Government **Giovanni Botero**	31
5	Inequality and Stability **Jean Bodin**	35
6	A Discourse on the Origin of Inequality **Jean-Jacques Rousseau**	40
7	Civil Government is for Defence of Rich Against Poor **Adam Smith**	53
8	Of the Origin of Ambition and of the Distinction of Ranks **Adam Smith**	59
9	The Origin of the Distinction of Ranks **John Millar**	73
10	Parasitic and Productive Classes **Henri De Saint-Simon**	95
11	Aristocracy and the Lower Classes in England **Alexis De Tocqueville**	103
12	Of Property and the Labouring Classes **John Stuart Mill**	111
13	Obeisances, Titles and Class Distinctions **Herbert Spencer**	124
14	The Ruling Classes **Gaetano Mosca**	153

INTRODUCTION

As there are several good anthologies on social stratification in existence something ought, perhaps, to be said in justification for adding another. Luckily the answer is easy: namely, that the existing anthologies focus on contemporary cases and views, while neglecting the historical dimension, to which the present book is devoted. True, the well-known reader by Bendix and Lipset does contain extracts from older writers, but these constitute a small proportion of the whole and do not include some of the most interesting works. Often, moreover, the emphasis is on Marx, Veblen and Weber; which is understandable in view of the excellence and pertinence of these authors but none the less creates a need for a treatment which would amplify the historical view beyond the bounds of this trinity. The reason why no selections from them are included here is primarily to avoid duplication of easily accessible and well-known material. This applies above all to Marx, whose works are continually reprinted and often sold at subsidised prices. A number of cheap selections contain passages which are most relevant to the present theme. For the same reason I have left out Veblen, whose *A Theory of the Leisure Class* - the most relevant of his books to our topic - is widely known, easily and cheaply obtainable and often quoted.

The case of Weber is more complicated: his often quoted, fairly rounded-up but brief general formulations are not his strongest point. The greatness of Weber lies neither in methodology nor in explication and formulation of concepts, but in his unsurpassed skill in finding hidden connections and unravelling chains of historical causation through comparative analysis with the aid of casually sketched or implicit generalisations. Concern with class structure pervades all his works with the exception of the methodological and the few minor pieces such as a description of the stock exchange. In his *Agrarian Relations in Antiquity,* for instance, he tells us how the class structure in Greece and Rome affected and was affected by the changes in tactics and military organisation, how it was connected with the peculiarities of the economic system, the character of the cities; and how it contributed to the stultification of capitalism in the Ancient World. In his studies of China, India and Israel he shows the interplay between the structure of the economy, organisation of the state, the religion and the literary culture, in which stratification plays the key part. None the less, he produced no neat and well-rounded definitions or theorems about the nature and forms of stratification; and consequently it is difficult to find in his works passages which are sufficiently self-contained not to be misleading and yet do justice to his extraordinary powers of insight. So, since the limitations of space impose choice, I have decided to leave him out, despite my great admiration for his works.

Since the name of Marx comes first to most people's minds whenever social inequality and class struggles are mentioned, I must say a few words on how I view his contribution to our understanding of these phenomena; particularly as he has been left out solely for practical reasons. The mere fact that the present anthology contains excerpts from Aristotle, and that three-fourths of the authors included preceded Marx, proved that - contrary to his devotees' notions - Marx did not discover the importance, let alone the existence, of inequality and class conflicts. His famous dictum that 'all history is the history of class struggles' was a catchy phrase to put into the party manifesto; but, if treated as an exact proposition, it must be dismissed as nonsense because the historical records show people doing many other things besides engaging in class struggles. A more sober putting of the same idea is to say that in all societies which have left historical records class conflicts were going on in some form - which is perfectly true and was taken for granted by Aristotle, Machiavelli and Adam Smith. Marx himself, it must be remembered, never made the extravagant claims which his devotees stake out on his behalf. Writing to Weydemeyer, he thus characterises his contribution in this field:

... no credit is due to me for discovering the existence of classes in modern society or the struggle between them. Long before me bourgeois historians had described the historical development of this class struggle and bourgeois economists the economic anatomy of the classes. What I did that was new was to prove: (1) that the existence of classes is only bound up with particular historical phases in the development of production, (2) that the class struggle necessarily leads to the dictatorship of the proletariat (3) that this dictatorship itself only constitutes the transition to the abolition of all classes and to a classless society.

(From Marx's letter to J. Weydemeyer of 5 March 1852)

Here Marx does not do justice to himself because his real achievements lie elsewhere; and if his contribution to our understanding of social inequalities were what he says, it would amount to nothing, boiling down to an unsupported prophecy, confirmed by nothing that happened since it was proffered. There is an analogy here to the problem of the merits of dialectical materialism. Even leaving aside its esoteric philosophical aspects, it is utterly untenable as a scheme for interpreting history if treated as a dogma, according to which the mode of production determines other aspects of culture without being subject to reciprocal influences. Indeed, the Marxists themselves conspicuously demonstrate that they do not believe in it when they seek or use political power to change the economic structure. In contrast, viewed as a methodological directive to try to relate beliefs, laws and institutions to economic conditions, Marx's formula has been extraordinarily fruitful. Nowadays the stress on economic determinants of everything is commonly overdone - and its latter-day devotees have pushed it to absurd lengths - but in the middle of the last century the economic interpretation of history was a great step forward. To appreciate its merits we must bear in mind that in that epoch at least 99 per cent of publications on history consisted of accounts of the doings of the great - their battles, pacts, intrigues, amours, squabbles and peculiarities, written with a eulogistic, chauvinistic and theological slant. Economic history did not exist at all, while any attempt to relate political actions (let alone religious beliefs) to economic conditions was regarded as blasphemy. By exaggerating and mixing scientific insights with the potent stimulant of political fervour, Marx succeeded in attracting attention to these problems; and thus became one of the founding fathers of economic history as well as sociology. True - as the reader of the present book can see - John Millar clearly practised the economic interpretation of history, but he did not formulate it as a doctrine, and consequently failed to attract attention and talent to it.

If we take the personalised and 'idealistic' (in the sense of idealised) conventional historiography of the nineteenth century as the thesis in the scheme of Hegel's dialectic, we can regard the 'materialistic' interpretation as the antithesis, and the balanced approach of Max Weber as the synthesis. The one-sidedness of Marx, Engels and their early followers amounted to a justifiable overshooting which corrected the opposite one-sidedness of the prevailing viewpoint and provoked a fruitful debate, which has eventually made possible a much better understanding of social causation. The same can be said about Marx's contribution to the study of the inequalities of classes. He added nothing to the stock of concepts in this field. The idea of defining a class on the basis of its relationship to the means of production is in Ricardo and Adam Smith; while the distinction between a class 'by itself' and 'for itself' is a purely scholastic sophistry as it stands. His real merit consisted of an over-emphasis which acted as an antidote to the prevailing oversight or wilful ignorance, if not camouflage; and which has been fruitful to the extent to which it provided a directive for research, accompanied by fascinating demonstrations on concrete cases of how it can be done.

The afore-mentioned directive can be analysed into the following precepts:
(1) ascertain the main economic interests;
(2) delineate groups on this basis;

(3) find out how the political groupings and programmes serve these interests;
(4) unmask the methods by which ideologies, programmes and religions camouflage this subservience.

This kind of approach has become familiar (and its exaggerations so obvious) that it is difficult to envisage how novel and illuminating it was when first applied. Despite various errors, Marx's treatment of the class struggles in France or Engels' of the Peasant War in Germany - to mention just two examples - constituted milestones in the development of political and sociological analysis: and the same could be said about the work of some of their immediate followers like Karl Kautsky and Antonio Labriola.

When analysing a concrete case Marx did not obey his own principle of distinguishing classes solely on the basis of a different relationship to the means of production, but also used the common-sense criterion of the amount of wealth, the rank in the hierarchy, and the way of life in accordance with which he distinguished the landowners from the businessmen, the big bourgeois from the small, the high nobility from the gentry, the rich peasants from the poor, the officer corps from the civilian functionaries - admitting that they may have divergent interests. Likewise, the value of his generalisations about the evolution of the class structure lies less in their correctness (which leaves much to be desired) than in the general principle of trying to relate this evolution to the changes in the economic system.

The famous 'law of the increasing misery of the proletariat' - to take the first example of such a generalisation - was a simple extrapolation of the trend of wages around the middle of the last century in England and France. Luckily for the proletariat but unluckily for the 'law', this trend was reversed just about the time of the publication of the first volume of *Das Kapital*. The thesis about the disappearance of the middle class and the polarisation of the class structure is more interesting: firstly, because it was in one sense confirmed and in another refuted by events; and secondly, because it is more than a simple extrapolation, being in fact derived from the 'law of concentration'. The validity of the latter is also ambiguous: it is confirmed in respect of the scale of production and control over it, while being refuted by the reality of the concentration of ownership of the means of production, which is no more advanced today than it was when this prediction was made. Concentration of control could proceed without a corresponding trend in ownership because of the advent of the joint-stock company, the importance of which Marx failed to appreciate, imagining that factories would continue to be owned by single masters - only fewer and bigger. Furthermore, although the middle class which Marx knew - which consisted of independent craftsmen, shopkeepers and farmers - has radically declined in importance, its place on the middle rungs of the social ladder has been taken by functionaries, managers and technicians, many of whom have a share in the ownership of the means of production. Further stimulated by the tremendous expansion of the administrative machinery of the state, the growth of the new middle class (as it was baptised by the German sociologists at the turn of the century) produced a bulging of the social pyramid in the middle instead of the polarisation expected by Marx. I would claim that all the shortcomings of Marx's forecasts stem from his failure to take into account the phenomenon of bureaucracy, but his errors were very fruitful in their time and have stimulated many (if not the majority) of the most interesting sociological studies produced before about 1930.

Having considered the most important among the absent writers, let us look briefly at those included, beginning - of course - with Aristotle. What strikes one about him is the extraordinary subtlety of his approach. Indeed, he is more sophisticated than many sociologists and political scientists of today, and it is not until the eighteenth century that we find thinkers who have reached his level. That (like Plato) he was fully aware of the ubiquity and importance of class struggles goes almost without saying; but what calls for emphasis is that he was aware that these struggles assume various forms and depend on many factors. His treatment of the related phenomenon of revolution is a great deal less simplistic than most of the recent studies because, instead of assuming a single recurrent pattern or cause, it begins with a recognition that each type of political system has its characteristic weaknesses which circumscribe what kind of revolution is likely to occur. Among other things, Aristotle clearly noticed the connection between military organisation and class structure; and (as I have tried to show in *Military Organisation and Society*) his ideas can be reformulated as proper general propositions.

Neither Machiavelli nor Bodin nor Botero have approached the subject in an equally systematic way. Nevertheless, their writings are of considerable interest: firstly, because they supply fascinating narratives and unexpected factual sidelights; and secondly, because they show how the best minds of that era viewed social inequalities.

The most noteworthy point about the first excerpt from Adam Smith (taken from *The Wealth of Nations*) is his 'Marxist' view of the state as the engine of exploitation; which is not only perfectly compatible with, but actually reinforces, his liberal economic principle that it is desirable to reduce the sphere of governmental regulation to the minimum required to maintain order and peace. The second excerpt (taken from *The Theory of Moral Sentiments*) contains an extraordinary penetrating examination of the mental mechanisms involved in perpetuating inequalities, which has hardly been bettered in anything written since.

In Rousseau and John Millar we find early examples of the evolutionist approach in which the growth of inequality is viewed as accompanying the general progress of civilisation. But their emphases differ: while Rousseau bewails the loss of primeval innocence and equality, Millar believes in no lost paradise and on the whole views history as progress from savagery. Nor does he share Rousseau's error of postulating a pre-social existence for early men. Moreover, in his more general treatise *On the Origin of the Distinctions of Rank,* as well as in *The Historical View of the English Government,* Millar shows such a clear awareness of the influence of the economic conditions on politics, inequalities and other aspects of society, that we can regard him as the founder, or at least a forerunner, of the economic (or, if you like, materialist) interpretation of history.

Although the consequences of the exploitation of slaves and serfs by landowners had already been examined with amazing thoroughness by Charles Comte, Henri de Saint-Simon was the first to build a vision of social reform around the distinction between productive and parasitic classes, which in his interpretation did not coincide with the division between the rich and the poor; for, unlike Marx, he believed that there were productive rich as well as parasitic poor. Progress in the past depended, according to him, chiefly on the balance of power between the productive and the parasitic classes; and the main feature of socialism (which term he invented) was the elimination of the latter and the creation of a society of producers. These points may easily be misunderstood when reading him today because he used the words *'les industriels'* (usually translated as 'the industrialists') not in the present sense of the leaders of large scale industrial undertakings but as the opposite of *'les oisifs'* (the idle) and comprising everybody engaged in manufacturing. Far from losing its relevance, Saint-Simon's thesis fits very well the world of today where there are proportionately more parasites than ever before in history, esconced in private as well as public bureaucracies, and in all kinds of parasitic and harmful occupations such as public relations, advertising and spurious education. Marx rendered a great disservice to the progress of our understanding by replacing Saint-Simon's distinction by a simplistic dichotomy where only the manual workers are counted as productive while the rest are regarded as exploiters. By other means the economists, beginning with Ricardo, have also helped to eliminate the distinction between the productive and the parasitic classes or groups from the mental horizons of the students of society.

Not much needs to be said about the extracts from de Tocqueville or Mill, the most general characteristic of which is that they illustrate a full awareness of the importance of the phenomenon of class, and of its interwoven-ness with other aspects of social structure. Tocqueville, moreover, clearly perceived the part played in history by circulation of élites — to use the expression coined much later by Pareto, who made this problem into the cornerstone of his system of sociology.

Although in the chronological order followed in the present book Spencer comes earlier than Mosca, I shall leave the former until the end and make a few comments about the Italian. Like his rival, Pareto, but without the latter's pompousness and pseudo-scientific pretensions, Mosca supplies a conservative refutation of Marx. Whereas hypocritical or blinkered conservatives pretend or believe that nasty things like class struggles do not exist — and in Britain and the United States have succeeded in keeping Marx under the carpet for decades — these Italian opponents of radical changes and defenders of private enterprise fully accepted the ubiquity of class conflicts but maintained that there is little scope for improvement in this respect because all that a revolution can achieve is to replace the old ruling class by a new. Pareto ruled out the possibility of a radical change in this respect, although he did say that economic improvement (that is, growth of wealth *per capita*) fostered greater liberties for the populace. Mosca's stated preference was for a situation of a balance of power between classes which would prevent the most extreme forms of oppression. They both argued around the turn of the century that any attempt to implement Marxism and achieve perfect equality would inevitably lead to an increased inequality of power, and consequently to an even greater iniquity.

It is often said that the essence of science is the discovery of a unity underlying apparent variety; and by this criterion Spencer's analysis of the symbols of deference ranks very high. Indeed, this relatively small piece from his *Principles of Sociology* achieves as much as Veblen's deservedly renowned book, *A Theory of the Leisure Class*. The merit of the latter work lies in explaining a large number of apparently arbitrary customs and usages, which on the surface have nothing in common, in the light of the principle of conspicuous waste: namely, that they serve the purpose of displaying the performer's status by showing that he does not need to work and can afford waste. Although (just as with Freud's theory of dreams and mistakes) no conclusive proofs can be given, the argument carries conviction as soon as it is stated because it makes so many incidents in everybody's experience fall into place. Likewise, it is difficult to resist the persuasive force of Spencer's interpretation of a large number of apparently disparate and senseless ceremonies as alternative manners of symbolising and ritualising the most primeval form of dominance and exploitation: namely, physical overpowering, enslavement and robbery. Even if there are exceptions, so many customary movements and expressions fit this thesis that it must be judged as extraordinarily illuminating.

The view of stratification as essentially a pecking order — where position is determined by relative power, while the notions and symbols of status exist as external manifestations of dominance — submission relationships — subsumes rather than contradicts the economic interpretation of social inequality because wealth is a form of power: over people not things. One can regard wealth as something separate from other forms of power only if one forgets that ownership is a relationship between the owner and other people, which determines who can use and dispose of certain objects designated as the property of the owner. The thing enters into no relationship with human beings: a car does not differentiate between being driven by its owner or a thief — it is people who react differently. Thus again we see that, if sifted and interpreted with a proper mixture of sympathy, respect and criticism, the insights of the great thinkers of the past can be made to fit together into a coherent whole — which shows that, despite vagaries and retrogressions, there is a certain cumulation of knowledge in the study of society.

1 REVOLUTION AND THE CLASS STRUCTURE

Aristotle

... the sedition will either be started by persons who envy the honours of those who have won success, or be due to the refusal of the latter to remain on a footing of equality when they feel themselves superior.

Revolutions also occur when the sections of the state which are usually regarded as antagonists - for example, the rich and the common people - are equally balanced, with little or nothing of a middle class to turn the scale; for where either side has a clear preponderance, the other will be unwilling to risk a struggle with the side which is obviously the stronger. . . .

Political revolutions are sometimes achieved by force, and sometimes by fraud. . . .

In democracies changes are chiefly due to the wanton licence of demagogues. This takes two forms. Sometimes they attack the rich individually, by bringing false accusations, and thus force them to combine (for a common danger unites even the bitterest enemies): sometimes they attack them as a class, by egging on the people against them. The result of such action may be seen in a number of instances. At Cos democracy was overthrown by the rise of discreditable demagogues and the combination of the notables against them. . . .

At Heraclea democracy was ruined by the behaviour of demagogues soon after the colony was founded. They treated the notables unjustly, and drove them out by their conduct; but the notables gathered their forces, returned, and overthrew the democracy. At Megara, too, democracy was ruined in a similar way. The demagogues, anxious to have an excuse for confiscating their property, drove a number of the notables into exile, with the result that the exiles became so numerous that they effected their return, defeated the people in battle, and established an oligarchy. The same fate also befell the democracy at Cyme, which was overthrown by Thrasymachus. A survey of the changes in most of the other Greek states is sufficient to show that they have generally been of this character [i.e. changes from democracy to oligarchy due to the action of demagogues]. Sometimes the demagogues, anxious to win popular favour, drive the notables to combine by the injuries they inflict in imposing public burdens - burdens which either force them to break up their estates or [at any rate] cripple their revenues. Sometimes they bring false accusations in the courts, in order to be in a position to confiscate the property of the wealthier citizens. . . .

There are two particular, and most obvious, methods by which changes are brought about in oligarchies. One is the unjust treatment of the masses by the government. Any leader is then an adequate champion, especially when it so happens that the leader comes from the ranks of the governing class itself. This was the case with Lygdamis of Naxos, who afterwards made himself tyrant of the island. Sedition which begins in a movement of resistance *outside* the governing class may take several different forms. Sometimes an oligarchy is undermined by persons who themselves are wealthy, but who are excluded from office. This happens when the holders of office are a very limited number; it has happened at Massilia, at Istros, at Heraclea, and in other cities. . . .

Oligarchies are disturbed from *inside* when their members themselves play the demagogue, for reasons of personal rivalry. They may do so in two different ways. One way is to practise the art of the demagogue on the governing body itself. . . . The other way in which the members of oligarchies can play the demagogue is by practising on the masses. This was the case at Larisa, where the police magistrates paid their court to the masses because they were elected by them; and it generally happens in all oligarchies where the magistrates - instead of being elected on a franchise limited to those who are eligible for office themselves - are elected on a broad franchise, including all the army or even the whole of the people, but with eligibility limited to the owners of large properties or the members of political clubs. (This used to be the rule at Abydus.) We may add that similar troubles also arise in oligarchies where the law courts are composed of persons not belonging to the sovereign civic body. When this is the case, men begin to practise the tricks of the demagogue in order to secure a verdict; and this leads to dissensions and constitutional change, as it did at Heraclea on the Black Sea. Troubles also arise when some of its members try to make an oligarchy still more exclusive; and those who champion equality of rights are then compelled to enlist the aid of the people.

Another way in which oligarchies may be disturbed from inside is when their members waste their substance in riotous living. Men who have done that want to create a revolution; and they either attempt to be tyrants themselves or set up some other person. Hipparinus set up Dionysius at Syracuse in this way. At Amphipolis a man of the name of Cleotimus [having lost his fortune] introduced Chalcidian settlers, and incited them after their settlement to make an attack on the rich. At Aegina, again, it was a similar cause [i.e. dissipation] which moved the man who conducted the transaction with Chares to attempt a change of the constitution. Men of this type will sometimes go straight for some attempt at political change: sometimes they stop short at embezzling the public funds; but even that leads to sedition eventually, whether the sedition be started by the culprits themselves or whether (as happened at Apollonia on the Black Sea) it is begun by those who oppose their misconduct. An oligarchy at one with itself is not easily overthrown from within. The constitution of Pharsalus may serve as an example: the governing body, restricted as it is, manages to control a large population because its members behave well towards one another.

Still another way in which oligarchies may be undermined from inside is when an inner oligarcy is created within the outer. Few as are the members of the whole citizen-body, even these few are not all admitted, in such a case, to the highest offices. This is what happened at one time in Elis. The constitution was already in the hands of a small body of senators; but it was only a very small handful of men who were ever appointed to the Senate. Its members, who were ninety in number, all held office for life; and they were elected, much like the Spartan senators, in a way which favoured the interests of a narrow range of families.

Changes may happen in oligarchies [owing to internal reasons, and without any attack from outside] alike in war and in peace. They happen in war when the members of an oligarchy are compelled by distrust of the people to employ an army of mercenaries. If a single man is entrusted with the command of these mercenaries, he frequently becomes a tyrant as Timophanes did at Corinth; and if the command is vested in a number of persons, they make themselves a governing clique. Fear of such consequences sometimes forces an oligarchy to employ a popular force, and thus to give the masses some share in constitutional rights. Changes happen in peace when the members of an oligarchy, under the impulse of mutual distrust, entrust the maintenance of internal security to mercenaries and a neutral arbiter - who occasionally ends as the master of both the contending factions. . . .

In aristocracies sedition may arise, among other reasons, from the limitation of office and honours to a narrow circle. This is a cause which . . . produces commotions in oligarchies; and it naturally affects aristocracies, because they too are in some sense oligarchies. In both types of constitutions - though for different reasons - the ruling class is small; and it is this common feature which will explain why an aristocracy may be regarded as a kind of oligarchy. Sedition due to this cause must particularly tend to arise when the mass of a people consists of men animated by the conviction that they are as good as their masters in quality. This was the case with those who were called the Partheniae at Sparta. They were the [illegitimate] sons of Spartan peers: they conspired together to vindicate their rights; but their conspiracy was detected, and they were sent out to colonize Tarentum. Sedition of the same kind may also arise when persons of great ability, and second to none in their merits, are treated dishonourably by those who themselves enjoy higher honours – as Lysander was by the kings of Sparta. It may happen, again, when a man of high spirit – like Cinadon, the leader of the conspiracy against the Spartan peers in the reign of king Agesilaus - is debarred from honours and office. It may happen, too, when some of the ruling class become excessively poor, and others excessively rich. This is a change which happens particularly in times of war. It happened, for example, at Sparta in the time of the Messenian War. ...

The actual downfall of aristocracies, and also of 'polities', is chiefly due to some deviation from justice in the constitution itself. In either case the origin of the downfall is a failure to combine different elements properly. In 'polities' the elements are democracy and oligarchy: in aristocracies they are both of these and the further element of merit; but even in the latter the real difficulty is that of combining the first two elements, which are the only elements that most of the so-called aristocracies (as well as 'polities') actually attempt to combine. The only difference between aristocracies and the constitutions called 'polities' consists in their different ways of mixing the same two elements; and this is also the reason why the former are less secure than the latter. Constitutions where the elements are so mixed that the tendency is more towards oligarchy are called aristocracies: those where the mixture is such that the tendency is more in favour of the masses are called 'polities'. This will explain why the latter are more secure than the former. The greater number forms a stronger support: and the masses are ready to acquiesce in a government when they have an equal share of power. It is different with men of considerable means. When the constitution gives them a position of superiority, they are apt to fall into arrogance and to covet even more. Generally, however, it may be said that if a constitution is not equally balanced, but is inclined in one or another direction, it will tend to change in that direction. The favoured element will proceed to increase its advantage: a 'polity', for instance, will change to democracy; and aristocracy will change into oligarchy.

It is possible, however, that change may also go in the opposite direction. Aristocracy may change, for example, into democracy, because the poorer classes, feeling themselves unjustly treated, may divert its natural tendency into the opposite direction; and 'polities' may similarly change into oligarchies, from the growth of a conviction that stability - the aim of every 'polity' - is only to be found under a system of proportionate equality, on the basis of desert, by which each man receives his corresponding due. It was a change of this nature [i.e. a change in the opposite direction] which happened to the aristocracy at Thurii. The first stage, due to reaction against the high property qualification required from holders of office, was a change to a lower qualification, coupled with an increase in the number of offices. The next stage, due to the fact that the notables had bought up illegally the whole of the land (the oligarchical bias of the constitution enabling them to indulge their greed), was the outbreak of civil war. Here the masses, becoming hardened in the course of hostilities, proved stronger than the civic guard; those who had more land than the law allowed were forced to relinquish their hold; [and the old aristocracy thus became a democracy]. We may add that the oligarchical bias present in all aristocratic constitutions has a general tendency to make the notables too grasping. In Sparta, for example, we see estates passing steadily into the hands of a narrow circle. ...

Constitutions generally may be undermined from without, as well as from within. This happens when they are confronted by a constitution of an opposite type, which is either their close neighbour or powerful even if distant. It happened in the days of the Athenian and Spartan empires. The Athenians everywhere put down oligarchies; the Spartans, in turn, suppressed democracy. ...

The causes of revolution and sedition in different constitutions have now been generally described. It remains to treat of the methods for preserving constitutions generally, and each type severally. We may begin with a general proposition. To know the causes which destroy constitutions is also to know the causes which ensure their preservation. Opposite effects are brought about by opposite causes; and destruction and preservation are opposite effects. On this basis we may draw a number of conclusions. The first is that in constitutions where the elements are well mixed there is one thing as vitally important as any - to keep a look-out against all lawlessness, and, more particularly, to be on guard against any of its petty forms. Lawlessness, when it takes such forms, may creep in unperceived - just as petty expenditures constantly repeated, will gradually destroy the whole of a fortune ...

This is one precaution which ought to be taken - to prevent the beginning of trouble in petty acts of lawlessness. Secondly, we may lay down the rule that confidence should never be placed in devices intended to hoodwink the masses. They are always exploded in actual experience. ...

Thirdly, we have to observe (and the observation is true of oligarchies as well as of aristocracies) that some states owe their stability not so much to the solidity of their constitutional systems, as to the good relations in which their officers stand alike with the unenfranchised and the members of the civic body. In such states the unenfranchised are never treated unjustly; on the contrary, their leading members are promoted to share in constitutional rights; and while the ambitious among them are not wronged on points of honour, the rank and file are not maltreated in matters of money and profit. Similarly, in these states, the officers and the other members of the governing class behave towards one another in a democratic spirit of equality. Democrats seek to widen the principle of equality until it is made to include all the masses. ...

The devices adopted ... for fobbing the masses off with sham rights are five in number. They relate to the assembly; the magistracies; the law courts; the possession of arms; and the practice of athletics. As regards the assembly, all alike are allowed to attend; but fines for non-attendance are either imposed on the rich alone, or imposed on the rich at a far higher rate. As regards the magistracies, those who possess a property qualification are not allowed to decline office on oath, but the poor are allowed to do so. As regards the law courts, the rich are fined for non-attendance, but the poor may absent themselves with impunity; or, alternatively, the rich are heavily fined and the poor are only fined lightly - as is the rule under the laws of Charondas. In some states a different device is adopted in regard to attendance at the assembly and the law courts. All who have registered themselves may attend; those who fail to attend after registration are heavily fined. Here the intention is to stop men from registering, through fear of the fines they may thus incur, and ultimately to stop them from attending the courts and assembly as a result of their failure to register. Similar measures are also employed in regard to the possession of arms and the practice of athletics. The poor are allowed not to have any arms, and the rich are fined for not having them. The poor are not fined if they absent themselves from physical training: the rich are; and so while the latter are induced to attend by the sanction of a fine, the former are left free to abstain in the absence of any deterrent.

The legal devices just mentioned are of an oligarchical character. Democracies have their counter-devices: the poor receive payment for attendance at the assembly and the law courts; the rich are not fined if they fail to attend. If we want to secure an equitable mixture of the two sides, we must combine elements drawn from both: in other words, we must both pay the poor for attendance and fine the rich for non-attendance. On this plan all would share in a common constitution: on the other, the constitution belongs to one side only. It is true that the constitution of a 'polity' or mixed state must be based on a citizen-body composed only of those who have arms and that this involves a property qualification. Even when they do not enjoy political privileges, the poor are ready enough to keep quiet, provided that they are not violently handled or deprived of any of their property. But moderation does not come readily; and those who enjoy political rights are not always humane to inferiors. There may, for example, be a difficulty in time of war. The poor are usually reluctant to serve, if they are given no subsistence allowance, and are thus left without any means. But if they are provided with subsistence they are willing enough to fight.

There are some constitutions in which the citizen-body includes not only those who are actually serving, but also those who have previously served. The Malian constitution, for example, in the south of Thessaly, gave the franchise to both; but it restricted eligibility to office to those who were actually on service. The first form of constitution which succeeded to monarchy in ancient Greece was one in which the soldiery formed the citizen-body. At first it consisted only of cavalry. Military strength and superiority were then the prerogative of that arm; infantry is useless without a system of tactics; and as the experience and the rules required for such a system did not exist in early times, the strength of armies lay in their cavalry. When, however, states began to increase in size, and infantry forces acquired a greater degree of strength, more persons were admitted to the enjoyment of political rights. For this reason [i.e. because there was then a notable extention of the franchise] the name 'democracy' was given at that time to constitutions which we now call 'polities'. It is not surprising that the old constitutions should have been oligarchical and, earlier still, monarchical. With their populations still small, states had no large middle class; and the body of the people, still few in number, and insignificant in organization, were more ready to tolerate government from above.

Source: from *The Politics of Aristotle,* trans. Ernest Barker (Clarendon Press, Oxford, 1946) pp. 215-25, 186-8.

2 ON INEQUALITY AND CORRUPTION

Niccolò Machiavelli

... it is vain to look for anything good from those countries which we see nowadays so corrupt, as is the case above all others with Italy. France and Spain also have their share of corruption, and if we do not see so many disorders and troubles in those countries as is the case daily in Italy, it is not so much owing to the goodness of their people, in which they are greatly deficient, as to the fact that they have each a king who keeps them united not only by his virtue, but also by the institutions of those kingdoms, which are as yet preserved pure.

In Germany alone do we see that probity and religion still exist largely amongst the people, in consequence of which many republics exist there in the full enjoyment of liberty, observing their laws in such manner that no one from within or without could venture upon an attempt to master them. And in proof that the ancient virtue still prevails there in great part, I will cite an example similar to that given above of the Senate and people of Rome. When these republics have occasion to spend any considerable amount of money for public account, their magistrates or councils, who have authority in these matters, impose upon all the inhabitants a tax of one per cent of their possessions. When such a resolution has been passed according to the laws of the country, every citizen presents himself before the collectors of this impost, and, after having taken an oath to pay the just amount, deposits in a strongbox provided for the purpose the sum which according to his conscience he ought to pay, without any one witnessing what he pays. From this we may judge of the extent of the probity and religion that still exist amongst those people. And we must presume that every one pays the true amount, for if there were not the case the impost would not yield the amount intended according to the estimates based upon former impositions; the fraud would then be discovered, and other means would be employed to collect the amount required. This honesty is the more to be admired as it is so very rare that it is found only in that country; and this results from two causes. The one is that the Germans have no great commerce with their neighbors, few strangers coming amongst them, and they rarely visiting foreign countries, but being content to remain at home and to live on what their country produces, and to clothe themselves with the wool from their own flocks, which takes away all occasion for intimate intercourse with strangers and all opportunity of corruption. Thus they have been prevented from adopting either French, Spanish, or Italian customs, and these nations are the great corrupters of the world. The other cause is, that those republics which have thus preserved their political existence uncorrupted do not permit any of their citizens to be or to live in the manner of gentlemen, but rather maintain amongst them a perfect equality, and are the most decided enemies of the lords and gentlemen that exist in the country; so that, if by chance any of them fall into their hands, they kill them, as being the chief promoters of all corruption and troubles.

And to explain more clearly what is meant by the term gentlemen, I say that those are called gentlemen who live idly devoting themselves to agriculture or any other useful pursuit to gain a living. Such men are pernicious to any country or republic; but more pernicious even than these are such as have, besides their other possessions, castles which they command, and subjects who obey them. This class of men abounds in the kingdom of Naples, in the Roman territory, in the Romagna, and in Lombardy; whence it is that no republic has ever been able to exist in those countries, nor have they been able to preserve any regular political existence for that class of men are everywhere enemies of all civil government. And to attempt the establishment of a republic in a country so constituted would be impossible. The only way to establish any kind of order there is to found a monarchical government; for where the body of the people is so thoroughly corrupt that the laws are powerless for restraint, it becomes necessary to establish some superior power which, with a royal hand, and with full and absolute powers, may put a curb upon the excessive ambition and corruption of the powerful. This is verified by the example of Tuscany, where in a comparatively small extent of territory there have for a long time existed three republics, Florence, Siena, and Lucca; and although the other cities of this territory are in a measure subject to these, yet we see that in spirit and by their institutions they maintain, or attempt to maintain their liberty; all of which is due to the fact that there are in that country no lords possessing castles, and exceedingly few or no gentlemen. On the contrary, there is such a general equality that it would be easy for any man of sagacity, well versed in the ancient forms of civil government, to introduce a republic there; but the misfortunes of that country have been so great that up to the present time no man has arisen who has had the power and ability to do so.

We may then draw the following conclusion from what has been said: that if any one should wish to establish a republic in a country where there are many gentlemen, he will not succeed until he has destroyed them all; and whoever desires to establish a kingdom or principality where liberty and equality prevail, will equally fail, unless he withdraws from that general equality a number of the boldest and more ambitious spirits, and makes gentlemen of them, not merely in name but in fact, by giving to them castles and possessions, as well as money and subjects;

so that surrounded by these he may be able to maintain his power, and that by his support they may satisfy their ambition, and the others may be constrained to submit to that yoke to which force alone has been able to subject them. And as in this way definite relations will be established between the ruler and his subjects, each will be maintained in their respective ranks. But to establish a republic in a country better adapted to a monarchy, or a monarchy where a republic would be more suitable, requires a man of rare genius and power, and therefore out of the many that have attempted it but few have succeeded; for the greatness of the enterprise frightens men so that they fail even in the very beginning. Perhaps the opinion which I have expressed, that a republic cannot be established where there are gentlemen may seem to be contradicted by the experience of the Venetian republic, in which none but gentlemen could attain to any rank or public employment. And yet this example is in no way opposite to my theory, for the gentlemen of Venice are so more in name than in fact; for they have no great revenues from estates, their riches being founded upon commerce and movable property, and moreover none of them have castles or jurisdiction over subjects, but the name of gentleman is only a title of dignity and respect, and is in no way based upon the things that gentlemen enjoy in other countries. And as all other republics have different classes under different names, so Venice is divided into gentlemen and commonalty, and the former have all the offices and honors from which the latter are entirely excluded; and this distribution causes no disorders in that republic, for the reasons elsewhere given. Let republics, then, be established where equality exists, and, on the contrary, principalities where great inequality prevails; otherwise the governments will lack proper proportions and have but little durability.

Source: from *The Prince and the Discourses,* trans. Luigi Ricci (Modern Library Series, Random House, New York, 1940) pp. 252-70.

3 CLASS STRUGGLES IN FLORENCE

Niccolò Machiavelli

The ineradicable hostility which naturally exists between the people and the nobles is caused by the one wishing to rule and the other to resist, and from this follows all the evils which arise in cities; for this contradictory spirit fosters everything which tends to disturb a commonwealth. This kept Rome ever at strife within herself, and if it is permitted to compare small things with great ones, this has caused the disunion of Florence, although the effects produced in the two cities have been very different. The dissensions which arose between the people and the nobles in Rome were settled at their commencement by discussion, whilst those of Florence were terminated by fighting. Those of Rome ended in a constitution, those of Florence in the death and exile of many citizens. The dissensions in Rome tended to increase the warlike qualities of her citizens, but in Florence they were entirely wiped out. Whilst the dissensions in Rome transformed the equality of her citizenship to the utmost inequality, those of Florence have reduced her citizens from a condition of inequality to a wonderful equality. The different ends which these two people set before themselves undoubtedly were productive of these very different effects. For the people of Rome were desirous of sharing the supreme honours with the nobles, whilst the people of Florence fought in order that they alone should govern without the participation of the nobles. . . .

The city . . . was divided into six wards which returned six signori, one from each ward, unless they chose, as sometimes happened, twelve or thirteen, but shortly after it was decreed that only six should be returned. To carry such a reform as the above it was found that six wards was not a convenient division, because it now being desirable to give a share in the representation to the nobles, it was necessary to increase the number of seats. Therefore they divided the city into four quarters, and gave three seats in the signoria to each. They abolished the office of gonfaloniere of justice and the standard bearers of the brotherhoods of the people, and in the place of the twelve protectors they created eight councillors, four from the nobles and four from the merchants. Having re-established the government on this basis the city would have been at peace if the nobles had been content to live with that moderation which is necessary in civil society; but they did the very opposite. As private persons they would not brook any equals, and as magistrates they insisted upon being masters. Thus every day there occurred some instance of their insolence and pride. The people were highly displeased at this, for they saw that for the one tyrant they had got rid of a thousand had risen in his place. Thus wrongs were increasing on one side and anger was rising on the other. Whereupon the merchants complained of the lawlessness of the nobles and their bad citizenship to the archbishop, and persuaded him to attempt to induce the nobles to resign their seats in the signoria and content themselves with other offices. The archbishop was naturally a good man, but easily led away by others, first to one side and then to another. Thus, at the instance of his colleagues, he had at first espoused the cause of the Duke of Athens, afterwards on the advice of some citizens he had turned against him. Then he had favoured the nobles in the re-organisation of the state, and now, moved by the reasons the merchants had given him, he was ready to help the people. Expecting to find in others his own want of firmness of mind, he easily persuaded himself that he could induce the nobles to agree to the suggestion, therefore he convoked the fourteen commissioners who had not yet laid down their office. In such language as he thought most suitable, he exhorted them to yield up their seats in the signoria to the people, and promised them that it would completely pacify the city, otherwise he feared that it and they would be ruined. This speech greatly incenced the nobles, and Messer Ridolfo di Bardi with harsh words rebuked the archbishop, telling him he was an unreliable man, reproaching him for his false friendship to the duke, and describing his share in the expulsion of the duke as treachery, concluded by saying that, as the nobles had gained their honours by the sword, so they would keep them by the sword. He then left the council chamber with his friends, and at once informed the other nobles of what was demanded of them. The merchants also declared their intention to their friends. Whilst the nobles were preparing to maintain their position in the signoria, the people determined to be beforehand with them, and rushed armed to the palace, shouting the demand for the resignation of the nobles. The tumult and noise was immense. The signori were abandoned, because when the nobles found the people ready armed they dared not take up arms, but shut themselves up in their own houses. The merchants first calmed the people by affirming that their colleagues among the signori were good modest men; but unable to arrange terms for them the signori were sent away to their own houses, which they only reached with great trouble. The nobles having left the palace, the four noble councillors were deprived of their office and replaced by twelve merchants. To the eight signori who remained was added a gonfaloniere of justice and sixteen standard bearers of the brotherhoods of the people, and thus the council was reformed so that the entire government of the city was vested in the people.

    Whilst these changes were taking place, a great famine occurred in the city which further intensified the feelings of the contending parties, the people being goaded by famine and the nobles by their loss of office. This state of affairs encouraged Messer Andrea Strozzi to make an attempt to capture the liberties of the city. This man sold his corn at a lower price than other merchants, and this occasioned a large concourse of people to assemble at his house. So one morning he was bold enough to mount his horse and with some of his retainers to ride through the city calling the people to arms, and in a very short time he had collected more than 4000 men. These he led to the Piazza of the signori, and demanded that the palace should be opened to him. But the signori with threats and force drove Strozzi and his men out of the Piazza, and afterwards so awed the people with proclamations that in a short time they had all retired to their houses. Strozzi being deserted by his followers fled, and with difficulty escaped falling into the hands of the magistrates.

This attempt, although it was rash and came to such a despicable end, inspired the nobles with the hopes of weakening the merchants, now that the lower classes were at strife with them. The nobles, therefore, availed themselves of this opportunity to arm themselves, in order to regain the rights which they considered had been unjustly taken away from them. They believed so confidently in victory that they openly fortified their houses, provided themselves with arms, and sent into Lombardy for assistance. The people and the signori also prepared for the struggle, arming and sending to Siena and Perugia for help. . . .

When in the time of Carlo I the city was divided into guilds, and a master and a constitution were given to each of them, it was provided that the members of each guild should be judged in all civil matters by the masters of these guilds. These guilds in the beginning, as we have said, numbered twelve, but afterwards they were increased to twenty-one, and had risen to such power that in a few years they absorbed the entire government of the city. Some being found to be of more or less importance than others, they were divided into greater and lesser guilds, of which seven were called the greater and fourteen the lesser. Out of this division and the causes related above, the arrogance of the captains of the wards took its rise, because those citizens who had formerly been Guelfs, and under whose government the magistracy was always sworn, had favoured the rich merchants of the greater guilds and had oppressed the members of the lesser ones. This caused the innumerable tumults of which we have spoken. In addition to this, many industries in which only small traders or the lower classes laboured had no guild of their own, but submission was yielded to one of the guilds which happened to assimilate in some degree to their own industry. Hence it followed that when these people became dissatisfied with their wages, or oppressed by their masters, they had no other course open to them but to appeal to the syndics of the guild to which they had submitted themselves, and from them they rarely received that justice to which they believed themselves entitled. And of all the guilds that had, and still have, most of that description of labour affiliated to them, the Guild of Wool is the most powerful and of the greatest authority, and it supports with its trade the greater number of the small traders and the labouring classes.

Thus it came about that the lower orders, not only those who were in submission to the Guild of Wool, but also those under other guilds, were full of resentment for the above reasons, and feared punishment for the burnings and robberies committed by them. Therefore they assembled at night to consider what could be done to meet the dangerous position in which they stood. One of the boldest and most experienced among them addressed them in the following words:

If we had now to decide whether we should take up arms, burn and pillage the houses of the citizens, and rob the churches, I should be the first among you to suggest caution, and perhaps to approve of your preference for humble poverty rather than risking all on the chance of a gain. But as you have already had recourse to arms, and have committed much havoc, it appears to me that the point you have now to consider is, not how shall we desist from this destruction, but how shall we commit more in order to secure ourselves. I believe beyond all question that, when nothing else can teach us, necessity will. On every side the city is full of complaints and hatred against us. The citizens are united on this point, and the magistrates are always consulting with the signori. Believe me, they are setting snares for us, and preparing fresh measures for coercing us. Therefore in our deliberations we ought to keep two things in view: firstly, to escape chastisement for what we have already done, and, secondly, to secure for ourselves in the future more liberty and more comfort. Let us begin, therefore, by insisting upon a pardon for the old offences, and to secure this pardon it is necessary to commit new offences by multiplying the plunderings and burnings and redoubling the disturbances, and above all let us increase the number of our comrades, because, where small faults are chastised, great crimes are rewarded, and where many men are involved no one is punished. When many suffer, few seek revenge, because where the injury is universal it is borne with more patience than when it is particular. The multiplication of offences, therefore, will enable us to obtain pardon more easily and put us in the way of obtaining those things which we need for our liberty. It seems to me that we shall most certainly get them, because those men who would stand in our way are both rich and disunited, and their disunion will give us the victory, and their riches, when we possess them, will enable us to keep it.

Do not let us fear that antiquity of blood of which they boast. Men have all the same beginning, nature casts them all in the same mould, and their blood is equally good. Strip us all naked, and you will find all are alike. Dress us in their clothes, and we shall be nobles beyond question; put them in ours, and they will appear commoners. It is only riches and poverty which make the difference between us. It grieves me to hear that some of you repent for conscience sake of what you have already done and wish to go no further with us. If this be true you are not the sort of men I thought you were, for neither conscience nor shame ought to have any influence upon you. Remember that those men who conquer never incur any reproach, and where there is, as with us, a dread of hunger and prisons, we should lightly esteem conscience with its apprehensions of hell. If you watch the ways of men you will see that those who obtain great wealth and power do so either by force or fraud, and having got them they conceal under some honest name the foulness of their deeds. Whilst those who through lack of wisdom, or from simplicity, do not employ these methods are always stifled in slavery or poverty. Faithful slaves always remain slaves, and good men are always poor men. Men will never escape from slavery unless they are unfaithful and bold, nor from poverty unless they are rapacious and fraudulent, because both God and Nature have placed the fortunes of men in such a position that they are reached rather by robbery than industry, and by evil rather than by honest skill. Hence it follows that men destroy each other, and he who can do the least injury always comes off worst. Therefore, you should always use your strength when you have the opportunity, and fortune never threw anything in your way better than your present chance, whilst the citizens are disunited, the signori hesitating, and the magistrates alarmed. Now is the time to conquer them, before they become united and find their courage. If we take this action we shall either become masters of the city, or we shall gain so much that not only will our past misdeeds be forgiven, but we shall be in a position to threaten fresh injuries. I confess this course is bold and dangerous, but when necessity drives audacity is the highest wisdom, and no courageous man takes any account of danger in great enterprises. For all undertakings that are commenced in danger are concluded in safety, and we can never avoid one danger without running into another. When we know that prisons, torments, and even death are being prepared for us, I believe there is more danger in remaining as we are than in seeking to make ourselves safe, because in the first case the perils are certain, and in the second case they are doubtful. How often have I heard you complaining of the cruelty of your masters and the injustice of your magistrates? Now is the time, not only to liberate yourselves from them, but to become so much their masters that they will have more to suffer and fear from you than you have ever had to endure from them. The opportunity flies that these chances have brought, and in vain will you seek to recall it when once it has passed. You see the preparations of our adversaries. Let us anticipate their plans, for doubtless those will be the victors who first draw the sword – they will succeed, and their enemies will be ruined. This course will bring honour to many of us and security to all.

These persuasive words set on fire the already inflamed minds of the people for mischief, and they decided to have recourse to arms as soon as they should have gathered together more of their fellows, and they bound themselves with oaths to support each other should any of them be hauled before the magistrate.

Whilst these fellows were maturing their plans to seize the republic, the plot was brought to the knowledge of the signori, owing to one Simone della Piazza falling into their hands and revealing to them the whole of the conspiracy. The danger was realised when it was learnt that the revolt was to take place on the following day, and the signori at once summoned the colleges and those citizens who, with the syndics of the guilds, were taking measures for the pacification of the city. It was evening before they could all assemble, and it was then advised that the consuls of the guilds should be sent for, and that every man-at-arms then in Florence should be ordered to assemble in the Piazza the first thing in the morning, and with them should come the gonfaloniere of the people. By chance, however, a person named Nicolo da San Friano was regulating the clock of the palace at the time when Simone was under torture and the citizens were assembling. Nicolo perceived at once what it all meant, and ran home, filling the whole neighbourhood with his cries, so that immediately more than a thousand men gathered in the Piazza of San Spirito. This uproar also reached the conspirators, and San Pietro and San Lorenzo, the places appointed by them, were quickly filled with armed men.

By this time the morning of 21 July had come, and there were not more than eighty men-at-arms assembled in the Piazza in reply to the summons of the signori, and none of the standard-bearers had arrived because, on learning that all the city was up in arms, they feared to leave their homes. The mob which first reached the Piazza came from San Piero Maggiore, and the men-at-arms made no movement on their arrival. Upon the heels of this mob followed another crowd who, finding no obstacle in their way, demanded with terrible shouts the release of the prisoners from the signori. Having failed to obtain the prisoners by threats they proceeded to force; they burnt down the house of Luigi Guiccardini, and compelled the signori to give their prisoners up for fear of worse happening. Having obtained them, the mob then wrested the standard of justice from the executioner, and marching under it proceeded to burn down the houses of those who were hated either on public or private grounds, for many citizens, merely to gratify their hate, led the mob against the houses of their enemies. So readily was this done that it was only necessary for a voice in the crowd to shout against such and such a house, or even for the man who carried the banner to point it in a certain direction. All the muniments of the Guild of Wool were also burnt. Having committed much destruction, the mob attempted to accompany it with the distribution of honours, and created Salvestro de' Medici and other citizens cavaliers, the number of which reached sixty-four. Among these cavaliers were Benedetto and Antonio degli Alberti, Tommaso Strozzi, and others who were in the confidence of the mob, but others were knighted against their will. It was to be remarked in these occurrences, and many did note it, that the mob burnt the houses of some of those whom shortly after they made knights, even on the same day, so quickly did honour follow the injury. This happened to Luigi Guicciardini, the gonfaloniere of justice. Amid this great riot the signori were completely disheartened at finding themselves deserted by their men-at-arms, the syndics of the guilds, and by the standard-bearers, none of whom had come, according to orders, to their assistance. Only two of the sixteen standard-bearers put in an appearance, namely those of the Lion d'Oro and Del Vajo under Giovenco della Stufa and Giovanni Cambi, and these left the Piazza very quickly when they found that none of the others followed them. On the other hand, many citizens, when they witnessed the fury of this roving multitude, and saw the palace abandoned, would not leave their homes. Some, however, followed the crowds of armed men in order to be in a better position to defend their own or the houses of their friends; and thus the power of the mob increased whilst that of the signori diminished. This tumult lasted the whole day, and when night came the mob stopped before the palace of Messer Stefano, which is situated behind the Church of San Barnaba. Their numbers exceeded 6000 men, and before daybreak they had compelled the guilds by threats to send them their banners. When morning came they marched to the Palace of the Podesta with the standard of justice and the banners of the guilds before them, and upon the podesta refusing to give up possession of the palace, they seized it.

Now that the signori discovered that they could not control the mob by force, they determined to make an attempt to come to terms with it. They therefore summoned four men from each of the colleges, and sent them to the people assembled at the Palace of the Podesta to learn from them what they wanted. These envoys found that the leaders of the people, with the syndics of the guilds and some other citizens, had already formulated what they intended to demand from the signoria.

Therefore, accompanied by four representatives of the people, the envoys returned to the signoria with these demands: — that the Guild of Wool should no longer maintain a foreign judge; that three new trade guilds should be established, one for the wool carders and dyers, one for the barbers, doublet makers, tailors, and such like mechanical trades, and one for the lower classes; that these three new guilds should always have two signori and the fourteen lesser guilds should have three signori; that the signoria should provide halls for these new guilds; that no members of the guilds should be called upon to pay debts under fifty ducats for the period of two years; that the pawn shops should cease charging interest and should only be repaid the principal; that all banished or imprisoned citizens should be pardoned; that all ammoniti should have their dignities restored to them. They demanded for their special favourites many other privileges besides these, and at the same time they called for banishment and imprisonment for those who had opposed them. Dishonourable and unjust as these demands were the signori agreed to them, fearing that worse might follow their refusal. As it was desirable that the demands should be ratified, the consent of the general council had to be obtained. But as both councils could not sit on one and the same day, it was agreed to wait until the following day. The mob now appeared satisfied, and the guilds content, and a promise was given that as soon as the laws should be passed all rioting should cease.

Whilst the general council was deliberating next morning, the multitude, all impatient and noisy, marched under their banners into the Piazza, and with terrifying shouts alarmed the council and the signori so much that one of their members named Guerrante Marignolli was so terrified that, on the pretence of making the doors safe below, he fled to his own house. He was not, however, able to steal away so secretly that the mob could not recognise him; but they did him no injury, only shouting out when they saw him that all the signori must leave the palace, and that if they would not do so then their children should be massacred and their houses burnt. In the meantime the laws had been confirmed and the signori had returned to their rooms; the council had descended the stairs and stood discussing matters in the portico and court-yard, in despair of their city. For never was there seen such foul play in a multitude, or such craven fears in those who ought to have curbed and kept them in order. The signori also were sorely perplexed and in despair for the safety of the country, also at finding themselves abandoned by one of their own number, and at receiving no assistance, either of strength or counsel, from a single citizen. Whilst they remained in this state of uncertainty as to what they could or ought to do, Messer Tommaso Strozzi and Messer Benedetto Alberti, moved either by their ambition to become masters of the palace or possibly because they believed it to be the wisest course, advised the signori to yield to the turbulent populace and retire to their own houses. This advice, proferred as it was by those who had been largely leaders in the disorders, was rejected with scorn by Alamanno Acciajuoli and Nicolo del Bene, two of the signori. These gentlemen with some show of vigour said that others might yield if they wished, and it could not be helped, but as for themselves, they did not intend to yield up their authority until the time came for them to do so, unless they did it with their lives. This resolution only redoubled the anxieties of the signori and increased the rage of the people, until finally the gonfaloniere, wishing rather to get rid of his office than imperil his life, entrusted himself to the care of Messer Tommaso Strozzi, who safely conducted him to his own house. The other signori, in much the same manner, one after the other, deserted the palace, even Alamanno and Nicolo, when they found themselves alone, also fled, preferring to be considered prudent rather than brave. Whereupon the palace fell into the hands of the populace and of the Eight commissioners of war who had not yet laid down their office.

When the mob entered the palace a man named Michele di Lando, a wool carder, bore in his hands the standard of the gonfaloniere of justice. This fellow, bare-footed and with but little clothing, mounted the stairs with the mob following him, and when he reached the audience chamber of the signori turned to the multitude and said: 'You see the palace is yours, and the city is in your power. What do you wish to do now?' With a great shout they answered that he should be their signore and gonfaloniere, and that he might govern the city as he pleased. Michele accepted the government, and as he was a shrewd and intelligent fellow, made up his mind to pacify the city and put down the rioting. In order to keep the people occupied, and give himself time to turn round, he ordered that Ser Nuto, who had been intended for the post of bargello by Messer Lapo da Castiglionchio, should be sought for and brought before him. Those who stood around him at once set out on this commission. Desiring to commence his government with justice, as he had acquired it by favour, he caused it to be published that it was his command that all burning and pillaging should at once cease, and as a warning to the mob he set a gallows up in the Piazza. To make a beginning with the reform of the government he discharged the syndics of the guilds and elected fresh ones; he deprived the signori and the colleges of their offices and burnt the ballot boxes. As for Ser Nuto, he was carried by the mob into the Piazza, and hanged by one foot from the gallows; when this was done those near to him began to cut him in pieces, and in a moment there was nothing left of him but the hanging foot. The Eight commissioners for war, on their part, believing that they were the leading people in the city since the signori had been driven out of the palace, had designated a new signoria. When, however, this came to the knowledge of Michele he informed them that they must at once leave the palace, as he intended to show every one that he could govern Florence without their assistance. Afterwards Michele assembled the new syndics of the guilds and appointed a signoria, choosing for this purpose four members from the lower classes and two each from the greater and minor guilds. Besides this he made a new scrutiny and divided the government into three parts, one of which was to be concerned with the greater guilds, one with the minor, and one with the new guilds. He gave to Messer Salvestro de' Medici the revenue arising from the shops on the Ponte Vecchio, and reserved to himself the podestaship of Empoli. To the citizens who had assisted the plebeians he gave many favours, not so much as recompense for what they had done, but to secure their assistance for his defence in time to come.

It appeared to the mob that Michele in his scheme of government had been too partial to the great merchants, and had not given to the plebeians that share of power which was necessary to enable them to keep their hold of it, or even to defend themselves. Whereupon, with their usual audacity, they at once took up arms and rushed tumultuously into the Piazza with their banners flying, and called for the signori to descend into the Ringhiera and discuss with them the plans which they were proposing to make for their own security. Michele saw clearly their insolence, but had no wish to incur their anger. Therefore, while not agreeing with their demand, he strongly condemned the way in which they put it forward, and advised them to lay down their arms, and they would then obtain what the dignity of the signori would not permit them to yield under compulsion. At this the mob became enraged with the palace, and went off to assemble at Santa Maria Novella, where they elected eight leaders from among themselves, with ministers and other appointments that would bring them both dignity and consideration. Thus the city had two factions and was governed by two different sets of rulers. The leaders of the mob decided among themselves that the Eight should always be chosen from out of their guilds, and should reside in the palace with the signori, and that everything which the government of the city wished to do should be confirmed by themselves. They deprived Messer Salvestro de' Medici and Michele di Lando of all that had previously been bestowed upon them. They assigned to many of their followers offices and appointments, and salaries with which to maintain their dignities. Having closed their deliberations the mob sent two of their leaders to the signori with the demand that their decisions should be confirmed, with the hint that if consent were not freely given force would be used. These fellows discharged their commission to the signori with great boldness and insolence. They reproached the gonfaloniere for his ingratitude and want of respect in exchange for all the honours and dignities they had conferred upon him. Towards the end of their discourse, when they proceeded to threaten him, Michele could no longer endure their insolence, and mindful rather of the rank which he then filled than that from which he had sprung, he determined to curb their extraordinary insolence with extraordinary means, and drawing the sword which he wore at his die he severely wounded one, and then had both bound and thrown into prison.

When this occurrence came to the knowledge of the mob, it was beside itself with rage, and, believing that it would easily gain by arms what it could not gain otherwise, set out at once amid great tumult to attack the signori. Michele, on the other hand, knew well what would happen and decided to anticipate the mob, thinking that it was more glorious to attack his enemy outside than to await him within the walls of the palace and have to fly in shame and dishonour as had his predecessors. He therefore gathered together a great number of the citizens who were beginning to recover their sense and, mounted on horseback with many armed men at his back, sallied forth to Santa Maria Novella in order to fight the mob. The populace had, as we have seen, come to the same determination; and at the very time Michele was moving against them, they had left Santa Maria for the Piazza, and by accident each of the parties took different ways and did not encounter each other. When Michele returned to the Piazza he found that it had been occupied by the mob and the palace heavily attacked. He at once joined battle with the mob and overcame it, driving part of the enemy out of the city, and forcing the rest to lay down their arms or hide themselves. This advantage was gained and the tumults quieted entirely by the personal valour of the gonfaloniere, who in courage, prudence, and rectitude excelled all other citizens of that time, and deserves to be enrolled among those exceptional men who have conferred benefits on their fatherland. Had he been animated by either ambition or malignity, the republic would have completely lost its liberty, and would have fallen under a tyranny worse even than that of the Duke of Athens. But his conscience would never allow him to think of doing anything that was not for the general good, and his prudence enabled him to conduct the affairs of the republic in such a way that most of his party yielded to him, whilst he was able to overawe the rest by force of arms. This caused the populace to dread him, but the better class of artisans settled down to their business, thinking that it was very foolish of them, after lowering the pride of the nobles, to endure the foulness of the mob.

At the time when Michele obtained his victory over the mob a new signoria had already been elected, but among its members were two of such vile and low condition that the citizens determined not to endure such a disgrace. When the new signori entered upon their office on 1 September, the Piazza happened to be full of soldiers, and a tumult arose as the late signori appeared outside the palace, and a great shout was raised that they would not have signori chosen from the lower class. Therefore the signori to satisfy them deprived the two men of whom we have spoken, Tira and Baroccio, of their seats and chose in their places Messer Giogio Scali and Francesco di Michele. The guilds of the lower classes were also abolished and their members were deprived of their offices, only Michele di Lando, Lodovico di Puccio, with some others of better quality being retained. The honours were divided, half going to the greater guilds and half to the lesser guilds. They decided that the signoria should consist of four members chosen from the greater guilds and five from the lesser ones, and that the gonfaloniere should be chosen first from one set of guilds and then from the other. This government secured some quietude for the city. But whilst the republic had been thus wrested from the hands of the lower classes, the artisan class had become far more powerful than the great traders. To this the latter yielded of necessity, in order that they might win over the lower classes from the lesser guilds by complying with their wishes. This was also the view of those who desired to keep under those men who as Guelfs had inflicted so many injuries upon the citizens. Among those who favoured this form of government was Messer Giorgio Scali, Messer Benedetto Alberti, Messer Salvestro de' Medici, and Messer Tomasso Strozzi, all of whom carried themselves like rulers in the city. The affairs of the city thus managed and ruled soon began to give rise to dissensions between the wealthy traders and the artisans, and these troubles were fostered by the rivalries of the Ricci and Albizzi. As from these dissensions there followed at sundry times the very gravest results, and as they will occur very often in our story, we shall call one the popular and the other the plebeian party. This form of government lasted three years and teemed with murders and banishments. For those who ruled lived in constant dread of the immense numbers of discontented people, both within and without the city. The malcontents within the walls were always attempting, or it was believed that they were, something against the rulers; whilst those who were outside, with no fears to restrain them, constantly raised trouble, first in one direction then in another, at one time through some neighbouring prince, at another through some republic. . . .

These dissensions did not end until the destruction of the government, which had ruled the city from the year 1371 until 1434, and which had carried on so many wars, conquered Arezzo, Pisa, Cortona, Livorno, and Monte Pulciano. Still greater renown would Florence have achieved if she had remained united and had not allowed those ancient strifes to be rekindled.

Source: from *Florentine History,* trans. W.K. Marriott (Everyman edn. Dent, London, 1909) pp. 99, 94-6, 116-27, 142.

4 CLASS AND GOVERNMENT

Giovanni Botero

THE THREE SORTS OF PEOPLE WHO MAKE UP THE POPULATION OF CITIES

In every state there are three sorts of people, the wealthy, the poor, and the middle class which lies between these extremes. The middle sort is usually the quietest and the easiest to govern, the two extremes are the hardest to govern, because the rich are drawn towards wrong-doing by the power that goes with wealth, while the poor are equally drawn to it by necessity. Solomon prayed to the Lord that he should neither be granted great wealth nor be allowed to fall into extreme poverty. Moreover those who have great riches and are distinguished by their noble birth and influential position are too proud and highly bred to suffer subordination, while the needy are as ready to obey an evil command as an honest one. The former are given to violence and unruliness and will attack their neighbour openly, while the latter turn to underhand forms of villainy. The rich are reluctant to submit to rule because they are fortunate, and Plato was unwilling to provide a legal code for the Cyrenians when they asked him for one on the grounds that it would be difficult to give laws to people who were so fortunately situated. The needy cannot live within the law because necessity, which oppresses them, knows no law. The middle rank are sufficiently wealthy to have no lack of what is required by their station, and yet their affluence is not such as to tempt them into ambitious schemes. They are usually friends of peace, contented with their station and neither exalted by ambition nor prostrated by despair; as Aristotle says, they are most inclined to virtue. We may suppose, then, that these middle folk will be peaceful, and proceed to deal with the extremes and the problem of how they should be prevented from causing riots and rebellions. . . .

PRINCES OF THE BLOOD ROYAL

. . . Such is the power of jealousy and ambition over the minds of those dominated by them that they are deprived of their humanity and indeed almost of their human nature. When Alexander the Great set off on his Asiatic enterprise he caused all his relatives to be put to death. The

Turkish rulers put their brothers to death on succeeding to the empire, while Amurath III even butchered a concubine of his father's who was pregnant. The kings of Ormuz, before that kingdom came under Portuguese rule, used to deprive their relatives of their sight, and some of the emperors of Constantinople did the same. The kings of China, who were more humane, detested such cruelty and were content instead to confine those of the blood royal in noble and spacious quarters provided with every comfort and delight. The kings of Ethiopia do much the same, for they keep their relatives on a high and pleasant mountain called Amara; there they have to remain until fortune calls them to succeed to the throne. This mountain is so sheer that it is like an impregnable fortress: it can only be climbed by one very narrow path, and there is enough cultivable land on the summit to provide food for a large garrison, so that it is entirely safe from assault and cannot be starved out by a siege. . . .

But the cruelty of the Turks in killing their brothers and relatives, and of the Moors in blinding theirs, is far less safe: in other countries anyone who seeks honour and rule is only driven to sedition or armed rebellion by his own ambition, which may be ensnared or restrained or diverted elsewhere, but among the Moors and Ottomans such men are driven by the need to save their own lives as well as by ambition. Hence there is no country in which there have been so many revolutions or civil wars as there have been in Ormuz, Tunis, Morocco and Fez (which are Moorish) and among the Turks, as we may see from the wars between Bajazet and Isa, between Selim I and his father Bajazet II, between him and his nephew Alemschah, between Soliman and his son Mustapha, and between Selim II and his brother Bajazet, who finally fled to the court of Tahmasp King of Persia and was there killed by his host in return for a promised reward of a million in gold. When a man knows that whoever obtains the throne will put him to death he considers his own interests and raises an armed force with the assistance of subjects of the country or foreigners. Hence Selim I was wont to say that though he had put to death so many brothers, cousins, nephews and other relatives, he should be forgiven because any other Ottoman, however lowly, would have done the same on attaining that rank.

On the other hand, we may see that in the kingdoms of Spain, Portugal, and France, the principalities of Germany and the other states of Christendom, although there are many members of the royal family and many princes in succession to the throne, there are infinitely fewer wars and rebellions than among these more barbarous peoples; this is because cruel laws and customs make men cruel, while humane ones make them humane. What royal house exceeds that of Austria in the number of princes of the blood, brothers and cousins? Yet they have never violated the principles of mutual affection, nor disordered the state by their ambitions; indeed each of them is ready to yield his rights and claims to the others and they live together on the best of terms, like many bodies animated by one spirit and governed by a single will. . . .

This cruelty of the rulers towards their relatives seems to me the most likely possible cause of the future downfall of the Turkish Empire, for since the Ottomans can marry as many wives as they wish and therefore have innumerable children, all of whom are certain to be killed by whoever succeeds to the empire, it seems inevitable that in the end internal war will arise which will weaken and divide the Empire and thus enable its enemies to attack and conquer it. . . .

OF THE POOR

Those who have nothing to gain from public peace, that is to say those who live in great poverty and wretchedness, are also a danger to it; for having nothing to lose, they are easily stirred by new events and willingly embrace any means that presents itself of bettering themselves by the downfall of others. Thus in Rome the poor (known as the fifth class) were not normally enrolled in the militia, except in the naval arm, which was regarded as less honourable than the land forces. Livy writes that when there were rumours in Greece of a war between King Perseus and the Romans, the poor were for Perseus because they hoped that everything would be overturned, while the wealthier citizens, who wished nothing to change, were on the side of the Romans. . . . And when Caesar aspired to rule his fatherland he looked to all those who had fallen into great necessity, whether through debts or bad management or some other cause, for since they had no reason to be content with the existing régime he thought them suited to his own purpose of overturning the state. There were some who were so poor that he could not help them, but he used to say openly of those that 'they needed a civil war'. . . . Those who are most ready to do evil are poor men who have been rich, and extreme poverty is as dangerous in a man of reputation and authority as extreme wealth. When David fled from the anger of Saul, and everyone that was in distress, and everyone that was in debt, 'and everyone that was discontented, gathered themselves unto him'.* The great troubles in France, the sound of which has been heard even here, have arisen from the same sort of people, for the rulers have become poor and fallen into heavy debts through the wars between the Most Christian and the Catholic kings, and the soldiers too have lacked the means to live and spend as they were accustomed to; thus both formed the plan of enriching themselves with the wealth of the Church, which in that country has a revenue of above six million crowns. Taking advantage of heresy (which they call 'the new religion'), they had recourse to arms, and thereby have reduced

* I Samuel 22:2

to extreme poverty what was once a flourishing kingdom. . . .

The ruler should either himself provide the poor with some means of livelihood, or make others do so. Dionysius of Halicarnassus says that nothing is more dangerous to a prince than an idle populace. To this end Augustus Caesar caused many buildings to be erected and encouraged the leading citizens to do the same, to keep the poorer elements in tranquillity. When an engineer proposed to Vespasian a method for transporting large columns to the Capitol at little expense, the Emperor rewarded him and said that he was pleased with the invention but preferred to have some way of giving a livelihood to the populace; meaning to say that he was willing to spend money in order to give a means of living to many who would have been deprived of it by this ingenious discovery.

Finally, the ruler should attempt to secure tranquillity by entrusting power only to those whose interests are bound up with internal peace and endangered by unrest and change. Thus Q. Flamininus, when he undertook the reorganisation of the cities of Thessaly, gave most power to the class which realised that the safety and tranquillity of the state would be to its own advantage.

Source: from *The Reason of State,* trans. P.J. and D. P. Waley (Routledge & Kegan Paul, London, 1956) pp. 82-94.

5 INEQUALITY AND STABILITY

Jean Bodin

... The conversion of a popular state into an aristocracy is generally the result of defeat in battle, or some other notable injury at the hands of an enemy. On the other hand a popular state is secured and strengthened by victory. These tendencies are illustrated in the histories of two commonwealths, Athens and Syracuse. The Athenians, who till then had enjoyed a popular form of government, having been defeated by the Syracusans through the fault of their captain, Nicias, fell under the dominion of four hundred citizens, though by a trick of Pisander they were known as the Five Hundred. When the humbler citizens tried to resist, they were overcome because the four hundred could dispose of the armed forces, and used them to kill the leaders and keep the rest in awe. But the Syracusans, puffed up by victory, destroyed their aristocracy and set up a popular state. A little later, the Athenians, on learning of the defeat of the Spartans by Alcibiades, killed or expelled their four hundred rulers and restored the popular state under the leadership of Thrasilus. ... We read also that the Florentines, on hearing of the sack of Rome and the captivity of Pope Clement,* at once got rid of the oligarchy that he had established in Florence. They persecuted, killed, or banished the partisans of the Medici, threw down their statues, broke open their treasuries, expunged their names from all buildings in the city and re-established the popular state. Again, the moment the Swiss Cantons had defeated the nobles in the battle of Sempach in 1377, there was no more heard of an aristocracy, nor of recognizing the Emperor in any form whatsoever. The reason for a revolution of this sort is the inconstancy and rashness of a populace, without sense or judgement, and variable as the winds. It is stunned by defeat and insupportable in victory. No enemy is more fatal to it than success in its own undertakings, no master so wise as the one that imposes the severest restraints on it, in other words, a victorious enemy. In such a crisis the wiser and richer citizens on whom the greatest burden falls, seeing dangers threaten from all sides, take the conduct of affairs, abandoned by the people, into their own hands. Indeed, the only way to secure the continuance of a popular state is to keep it at war, and create enemies if they do not already exist. This was the chief reason which led Scipio

---

* A Medici who governed Florence through the Cardinal Passerini. Hence the outbreak against the régime when the Pope became a prisoner in Castel Sant' Angelo in 1527 when Rome was sacked by the Imperial army under the Constable de Bourbon.

the Younger to try and stop the razing of Carthage. He had the wisdom to foresee that a warlike and aggressive people like the Romans would fall to making war on each other, once all external enemies were disposed of . . . . But popular states are more likely to change into monarchies as a result either of civil war, or of the folly of the people in giving too much power to an individual. . . .

On the other hand when a tyranny is overthrown as a result of a civil war, it is nearly always succeeded by a popular state. This is because the people know no moderation, and once the tyrant is expelled, the hatred of his memory, and the fear of once again falling a victim, excites them to rush to the other extreme. . . This happened in Rome after the expulsion of Tarquin the Proud, and in Switzerland, once the Imperial Vicars were killed, the people established a popular state which has lasted till the present day, that is to say for two hundred and sixty years. . . .

It also sometimes happens that a people is so unstable that it is impossible to find any form of government with which it does not become discontented after a brief experience of it. The Athenians . . . the Florentines and the Genoese were like this. The minute they had established one form of government, they began to long for another. This malady particularly affects those popular states whose citizens are of an active and enquiring turn of mind, as were those whom I have mentioned. Each citizen thought himself fitted to command the rest. When the citizens are of a less restlessly intelligent type they submit complacently to being ruled, and are easily brought to a decision in their public assemblies. More subtle spirits argue the point till intention evaporates in words. Personal ambition prevents anyone deferring to his opponent, and the state is thereby brought to ruin. It is a matter of common knowledge that Florence is the nursery of ingenious spirits. How much the Florentines differ from, say, the Swiss in this respect. Nevertheless though both peoples substituted a popular state for a monarchical form of government about three hundred and sixty years ago, while the Swiss have preserved their popular institutions . . . the Florentines have never ceased to change and change again, behaving like the sick man who keeps on moving from one place to another, thinking thus to cure the illness which is attacking his very life. In the same way the malady of ambition and sedition never ceased to afflict Florence until a physician was found to cure her of all her ills. A monarch succeeded who built fortresses in the city, garrisoned them strongly, and by such methods maintained a government which has lasted for forty years now.* . . .

Aristocratic states are more stable and longer lived than popular

---

* Duke Cosimo I de'Medici, 1537–74.

ones, provided that the ruling class avoid the two dangers of faction within their own ranks, and attack from a rebellious populace outside them. If they once start to dispute amongst themselves, the people will never fail to seize the opportunity to fall upon them, as the history of Florence shows only too well. This danger is intensified when foreigners are freely admitted into the city and settle in large numbers. Not being qualified for office, when they are heavily taxed or oppressed in any way by the governing body, their ready remedy is to rise and expel the native rulers. This is the danger which most threatens the state of Venice. It is a pure aristocracy. But it has admitted foreigners in such numbers that by now for every Venetian gentleman there are a hundred citizens, both nobles and burgesses, of foreign extraction.

The change from aristocracy to popular state has nearly always been bloody and violent. On the other hand the reverse process of change from popular state to aristocracy nearly always comes about gradually and peacefully. This happens when a city admits foreign settlers who in course of time considerably increase in numbers, but who remain ineligible for office or political rights. The strain of government and of war brings about a gradual diminution in the ruling class, whereas the number of aliens steadily increases. A point is reached when it is only a minority of the inhabitants who enjoy rights of sovereignty, and this, we have shown, is the distinguishing mark of an aristocracy. The commonwealths of Venice, Lucca, Ragusa, and Genoa were all once popular states which have gradually and insensibly been converted into aristocracies. The change was further facilitated, of course, by the reluctance of the poorer citizens, who needed all their time and energy to make a living, to accept public duties to which no profit was attached. In course of time, and by prescription, their families have lost the right to such offices altogether.

This type of revolution is the easiest and least insupportable of any. But if one wishes to prevent it happening, the children of immigrants must be admitted to public charges and offices, unless there are very urgent reasons why not, especially if the commonwealth is much involved in wars abroad. Otherwise there is the danger that the ruling class, not daring to arm its subjects, will be destroyed by defeat in battle, whereupon the people will seize power . . . The thing that most assisted the victory of the Roman people over the nobles was the defeat of the latter by the men of Viei, for the greater part of the gentry were killed, including three hundred members of the most ancient and noble family of the Fabii. The Venetians solve this problem by employing foreign mercenaries as a general rule, if they have to make war, though they avoid doing so whenever possible.

This danger of a revolution in the form of the state, following the destruction of the nobles, does not afflict monarchies, except in the extreme case of all Princes of the Blood perishing with the nobles. The Turks have seen to it that no single gentleman escaped in any province which they intended to annex. But this sort of change is rather the absorption of one state by another than a revolution in government and proceeds from external and not internal causes. But practically the entire noblesse of France was killed in the battle of Fontenoy near Auxerre, in the war between Lothar, son of Louis the Pious, and his brothers Louis and Charles the Bald. Nevertheless all three monarchies survived as such. . . .

Great and notable revolutions are most likely to befall aristocracies and popular states. There is no more common occasion than the ambition of proud men, who cannot obtain the rewards on which they have fixed their desires, and so constitute themselves the friends of the people and enemies of the noblesse. Thus did Marius in Rome, Thrasibulus in Athens, Francesco Valori* in Florence, and many others. This is all the easier to accomplish when unworthy persons are preferred to positions of honour and trust, and those who are worthy of them excluded. This angers men of birth and position more than anything else. What most contributed to the ruin of the Emperors Nero and Heliogabalus was the promotion of despicable persons to the highest honours. But this danger is greatest in an aristocracy governed aristocratically, that is to say where the generality of people have no share in office. It is a two-fold grievance to find not only that one is excluded from all offices and benefices, but that these are monopolized by unworthy persons to whom one must submit and do reverence. In such a case those patricians who can organize a following, can change an aristocracy which has no foundations in popular support, into a popular state. This cannot happen if the ruling class preserves its solidarity. Divisions and antagonisms within the ruling class is the danger most to be feared in the aristocratic state. . .

Revolutions tend to occur more frequently in small commonwealths than in those which are large and populous. A small commonwealth easily falls into two hostile camps. It is not so easy for such a division to appear in a large one, for there are always a number of people who are neither great nor humble, rich nor poor, good nor evil who form links between the extremes, because they have affinities with each. We find that the small republics of Italy and ancient Greece, consisting of one, two or three cities only, suffered many and diverse changes of form. There can be no question but that extremes always lead to conflicts if there is no means of uniting or reconciling them one with another. One can see at a glance the jealousy which divides noble and

---

* He supported Savonarola and the popular party against the aristocrats, and was set upon and killed by his enemies when Savonarola fell.

tradesman, the rich man and the poor man, the virtuous and the vicious. But more than this, one sometimes finds that the conflicting interests of different localities in the same city bring about a revolution. We read in Plutarch that the Republic of Athens was harassed by seditions and disorders because the sailors who inhabited the port were separated from those who lived near the Acropolis, and extremely hostile to them till Pericles included the port within his long walls. Venice was at one time in extreme danger from a similar conflict between the sailors and pilots on the one hand, and inhabitants of the city on the other, and but for the intervention of Pietro Loredano[1] would have suffered a violent revolution.

[1] Venetian admiral commanding in the wars of the early fourteenth century, victor over the Turks at Gallipoli in 1416, over the Genoese at Rapallo in 1431, and defender of Constantinople 1421-24.

Source: from *Six Books of the Commonwealth,* abridged and trans. M.J. Tooley (Basil Blackwell, Oxford, 1967) pp. 117-21.

6 A DISCOURSE ON THE ORIGIN OF INEQUALITY

Jean-Jacques Rousseau

The first man who, having enclosed a piece of ground, bethought himself of saying 'this is mine', and found people simple enough to believe him, was the real founder of civil society. From how many crimes, wars, and murders, from how many horrors and misfortunes might not any one have saved mankind, by pulling up the stakes, or filling up the ditch, and crying to his fellows: 'Beware of listening to this imposter; you are undone if you once forget that the fruits of the earth belong to us all, and the earth itself to nobody.' But there is great probability that things had then already come to such a pitch, that they could no longer continue as they were; for the idea of property depends on many prior ideas, which could only be acquired successively, and cannot have been formed all at once in the human mind. Mankind must have made very considerable progress, and acquired considerable knowledge and industry which they must also have transmitted and increased from age to age, before they arrived at this last point of the state of nature. Let us then go farther back, and endeavour to unify under a single point of view that slow succession of events and discoveries in the most natural order.

Man's first feeling was that of his own existence, and his first care of self-preservation. The produce of the earth furnished him with all he needed, and instinct told him how to use it. Hunger and other appetites made him at various times experience various modes of existence; and among these was one which urged him to propagate his species – a blind propensity that, having nothing to do with the heart, produced a merely animal act. The want once gratified, the two sexes knew each other no more; and even the offspring was nothing to its mother, as soon as it could do without her.

Such was the condition of infant man; the life of an animal limited at first to mere sensations, and hardly profiting by the gifts nature bestowed on him, much less capable of entertaining a thought of forcing anything from her. But difficulties soon presented themselves, and it became necessary to learn how to surmount them: the height of the trees, which prevented him from gathering their fruits, the competition of other animals desirous of the same fruits, and the ferocity of those who needed them for their own preservation, all obliged him to apply himself to bodily exercises. He had to be active, swift of foot, and vigorous in fight. Natural weapons, stones, and sticks, were easily found: he learnt to surmount the obstacles of nature, to contend in case of necessity with other animals, and to dispute for the means of subsistence even with other men, or to indemnify himself for what he was forced to give up to a stronger.

In proportion as the human race grew more numerous, men's cares increased. The difference of soils, climates, and seasons, must have introduced some differences into their manner of living. Barren years, long and sharp winters, scorching summers which parched the fruits of the earth, must have demanded a new industry. On the seashore and the banks of rivers, they invented the hook and line, and became fishermen and eaters of fish. In the forests they made bows and arrows, and became huntsmen and warriors. In cold countries they clothed themselves with the skins of the beasts they had slain. The lightning, a volcano, or some lucky chance acquainted them with fire, a new resource against the rigours of winter: they next learned how to preserve this element, then how to reproduce it, and finally how to prepare with it the flesh of animals which before they had eaten raw.

This repeated relevance of various beings to himself, and one to another, would naturally give rise in the human mind to the perceptions of certain relations between them. Thus the relations which we denote by the terms great, small, strong, weak, swift, slow, fearful, bold, and the like, almost insensibly compared at need, must have at length produced in him a kind of reflection, or rather a mechanical prudence, which would indicate to him the precautions most necessary to his security.

The new intelligence which resulted from this development increased his superiority over other animals, by making him sensible of it. He would now endeavour, therefore, to ensnare them, would play them a thousand tricks, and though many of them might surpass him in swiftness or in strength, would in time become the master of some and the scourge of others. Thus, the first time he looked into himself, he felt the first emotion of pride; and, at a time when he scarce knew how to distinguish the different orders of beings, by looking upon his species as of the highest order, he prepared the way for assuming pre-eminence as an individual.

Other men, it is true, were not then to him what they now are to us, and he had no greater intercourse with them than with other animals; yet they were not neglected in his observations. The conformities, which he would in time discover between them, and between himself and his female, led him to judge of others which were not then perceptible; and finding that they all behaved as he himself would have done in like circumstances, he naturally inferred that their manner of thinking and acting was altogether in conformity with his own. This important truth, once deeply impressed on his mind, must have induced him, from an intuitive feeling more certain and much more rapid than any kind of reasoning, to pursue the rules of conduct, which he had best observe towards them, for his own security and advantage.

Taught by experience that the love of well-being is the sole motive of human actions, he found himself in a position to distinguish the few cases, in which mutual interest might justify him in relying upon the assistance of his fellows; and also the still fewer cases in which a conflict of interests might give cause to suspect them. In the former case, he joined in the same herd with them, or at most in some kind of loose association, that laid no restraint on its members, and lasted no longer than the transitory occasion that formed it. In the latter case, every one sought his own private advantage, either by open force, if he thought himself strong enough, or by address and cunning, if he felt himself the weaker.

In this manner, men may have insensibly acquired some gross ideas of mutual undertakings, and of the advantages of fulfilling them: that is, just so far as their present and apparent interest was concerned: for they were perfect strangers to foresight, and were so far from troubling themselves about the distant future, that they hardly thought of the morrow. If a deer was to be taken every one saw that, in order to succeed, he must abide faithfully by his post: but if a hare happened to come within the reach of any one of them, it is not to be doubted that he pursued it without scruple, and, having seized his prey, cared very little, if by so doing he caused his companions to miss theirs.

It is easy to understand that such intercourse would not require a language much more refined than that of rooks or monkeys, who associate together for much the same purpose. Inarticulate cries, plenty of gestures, and some imitative sounds, must have been for a long time the universal language; and by the addition, in every country, of some conventional articulate sounds (of which, as I have already intimated, the first institution is not too easy to explain) particular languages were produced; but these were rude and imperfect, and nearly such as are now to be found among some savage nations.

Hurried on by the rapidity of time, by the abundance of things I have to say, and by the almost insensible progress of things in their beginnings, I pass over in an instant a multitude of ages; for the slower the events were in their succession, the more rapidly may they be described.

These first advances enabled men to make others with greater rapidity. In proportion as they grew enlightened, they grew industrious. They ceased to fall asleep under the first tree, or in the first cave that afforded them shelter; they invented several kinds of implements of hard and sharp stones, which they used to dig up the earth, and to cut wood; they then made huts out of branches, and afterwards learnt to plaster them over with mud and clay. This was the epoch of a first revolution, which established and distinguished families, and introduced a kind of property, in itself the source of a thousand quarrels and conflicts. As, however, the strongest were probably the first to build themselves huts which they felt themselves able to defend, it may be concluded that the weak found it much easier and safer to imitate, than to attempt to dislodge them: and of those who were once provided with huts, none could have any inducement to appropriate that of his neighbour; not indeed so much because it did not belong to him, as because it could be of no use, and he could not make himself master of it without exposing himself to a desperate battle with the family which occupied it.

The first expansions of the human heart were the effects of a novel situation, which united husbands and wives, fathers and children, under one roof. The habit of living together soon gave rise to the finest feelings known to humanity, conjugal love and paternal affection. Every family became a little society, the more united because liberty and reciprocal attachment were the only bonds of its union. The sexes, whose manner of life had been hitherto the same, began now to adopt different ways of living. The women became more sedentary, and accustomed themselves to mind the hut and their children, while the men went abroad in search of their common subsistence. From living a softer life, both sexes also began to lose something of their strength and ferocity: but, if individuals became to some extent less able to encounter wild beasts separately, they found it, on the other hand, easier to assemble and resist in common.

The simplicity and solitude of man's life in his new condition, the paucity of his wants, and the implements he had invented to satisfy them, left him a great deal of leisure, which he employed to furnish himself with many conveniences unknown to his fathers: and this was the first yoke he inadvertently imposed on himself, and the first source of the evils he prepared for his descendants. For, besides continuing thus to enervate both body and mind, these conveniences lost with use almost all their power to please, and even degenerated into real needs, till the want of them became far more disagreeable than the possession of them had been pleasant. Men would have been unhappy at the loss of them, though the possession did not make them happy. ...

As soon as men began to value one another, and the idea of consideration had got a footing in the mind, every one put in his claim to it, and it became impossible to refuse it to any with impunity. Hence arose the first obligations of civility even among savages; and every intended injury became an affront; because, besides the hurt which might result from it, the party injured was certain to find in it a contempt for his person, which was often more insupportable than the hurt itself.

Thus, as every man punished the contempt shown him by others, in proportion to his opinion of himself, revenge became terrible, and men bloody and cruel. This is precisely the state reached by most of the savage nations known to us: and it is for want of having made a proper distinction in our ideas, and seen how very far they already are from the state of nature, that so many writers have hastily concluded that man is naturally cruel, and requires civil institutions to make him more mild; whereas nothing is more gentle than man in his primitive state, as he is placed by nature at an equal distance from the stupidity of brutes, and the fatal ingenuity of civilized man. Equally confined by instinct and reason to the sole care of guarding himself against the mischiefs which threaten him, he is restrained by natural compassion from doing any injury to others, and is not led to do such a thing even in return for injuries received. For, according to the axiom of the wise Locke, 'There can be no injury where there is no property.'

But it must be remarked that the society thus formed, and the relations thus established among men, required of them qualities different from those which they possessed from their primitive constitution. Morality began to appear in human actions, and every one, before the institution of law, was the only judge and avenger of the injuries done him, so that the goodness which was suitable in the pure state of nature was no longer proper in the new-born state of society. Punishments had to be made more severe, as opportunities of offending became more frequent, and the dread of vengeance had to take the place of the rigour of the law. Thus, though men had become less patient, and their natural compassion had already suffered some diminution, this period of expansion of the human faculties, keeping a just mean between the indolence of the primitive state and the petulant activity of our egoism, must have been the happiest and most stable of epochs. The more we reflect on it, the more we shall find that this state was the least subject to revolutions, and altogether the very best man could experience; so that he can have departed from it only through some fatal accident, which, for the public good, should never have happened. The examples of savages, most of whom have been found in this state, seems to prove that men were meant to remain in it, that it is the real youth of the world, and that all subsequent advances have been apparently so many steps towards the perfection of the individual, but in reality towards the decrepitude of the species.

So long as men remained content with their rustic huts, so long as they were satisfied with clothes made of the skins of animals and sewn together with thorns and fish-bones, adorned themselves only with feathers and shells, and continued to paint their bodies different colours, to improve and beautify their bows and arrows, and to make with sharp-edged stones fishing boats or clumsy musical instruments; in a word, so long as they undertook only what a single person could accomplish, and confined themselves to such arts as did not require the joint labour of several hands, they lived free, healthy, honest, and happy lives, so long as their nature allowed, and as they continued to enjoy the pleasures of mutual and independent intercourse. But from the moment one man began to stand in need of the help of another; from the moment it appeared advantageous to any one man to have enough provisions for two, equality disappeared, property was introduced, work became indispensable, and vast forests became smiling fields, which man had to water with the sweat of his brow, and where slavery and misery were soon seen to germinate and grow up with the crops.

Metallurgy and agriculture were the two arts which produced this great revolution. The poets tell us it was gold and silver, but, for the philosophers, it was iron and corn, which first civilized men, and ruined humanity. Thus both were unknown to the savages of America, who for that reason are still savage: the other nations also seem to have continued in a state of barbarism while they practised only one of these arts. One of the best reasons, perhaps, why Europe has been, if not longer, at least more constantly and highly civilized than the rest of the world, is that it is at once the most abundant in iron and the most fertile in corn. ...

The cultivation of the earth necessarily brought about its distribution; and property, once recognized, gave rise to the first rules of justice; for, to secure each man his own, it had to be possible for each to have something. Besides, as men began to look forward to the future, and all had something to lose, every one had reason to apprehend that reprisals would follow any injury he might do to another. This origin is so much the more natural, as it is impossible to conceive how property can come from anything but manual labour: for what else can a man add to things which he does not originally create, so as to make them his own property? It is the husbandman's labour alone that, giving him a title to the produce of the ground he has tilled, gives him a claim also to the land itself, at least till harvest; and so, from year to year, a constant possession which is easily transformed into property. When the ancients, says Grotius, gave to Ceres the title of Legislatrix, and to a festival celebrated in her honour the name of Thesmophoria, they meant by that that the distribution of lands had produced a new kind of right: that is to say, the right of property, which is different from the right deducible from the law of nature.

In this state of affairs, equality might have been sustained, had the talents of individuals been equal, and had, for example, the use of iron and the consumption of commodities always exactly balanced each other; but, as there was nothing to preserve this balance, it was soon disturbed; the strongest did most work; the most skilful turned his labour to best account; the most ingenious devised methods of diminishing his labour: the husbandman wanted more iron, or the smith more corn, and, while both laboured equally, the one gained a great deal by his work, while the other could hardly support himself. Thus natural inequality unfolds itself insensibly with that of combination, and the difference between men, developed by their different circumstances, becomes more sensible and permanent in its effects, and begins to have an influence, in the same proportion, over the lot of individuals.

Matters once at this pitch, it is easy to imagine the rest. I shall not detain the reader with a description of the successive invention of other arts, the development of language, the trial and utilisation of talents, the inequality of fortunes, the use and abuse of riches, and all the details connected with them which the reader can easily supply for himself. I shall confine myself to a glance at mankind in this new situation.

Behold then all human faculties developed, memory and imagination in full play, egoism interested, reason active and the mind almost at the highest point of its perfection. Behold all the natural qualities in action, the rank and condition of every man assigned him; not merely his share of property and his power to serve or injure others, but also his wit, beauty, strength or skill, merit or talents: and these being the only qualities capable of commanding respect, it soon became necessary to possess or to affect them.

It now became the interest of men to appear what they really were not. To be and to seem became two totally different things; and from this distinction sprang insolent pomp and cheating trickery, with all the numerous vices that go in their train. On the other hand, free and independent as men were before, they were now, in consequence of a multiplicity of new wants, brought into subjection, as it were, to all nature, and particularly to one another; and each became in some degree a slave even in becoming the master of other men: if rich, they stood in need of the services of others; if poor, of their assistance; and even a middle condition did not enable them to do without one another. Man must now, therefore have been perpetually employed in getting others to interest themselves in his lot, and in making them, apparently at least, if not really, find their advantage in promoting his own. Thus he must have been sly and artful in his behaviour to some and imperious and cruel to others; being under a kind of necessity to ill-use all the persons of whom he stood in need, when he could not frighten them into compliance, and did not judge it his interest to be useful to them. Insatiable ambition, the thirst of raising their respective fortunes, not so much from real want as from the desire to surpass others, inspired all men with a vile propensity to injure one another, and with a secret jealousy, which is the more dangerous, as it puts on the mask of benevolence, to carry its point with greater security. In a word, there arose rivalry and competition on the one hand, and conflicting interests on the other, together with a secret desire on both of profiting at the expense of others. All these evils were the first effects of property, and the inseparable attendants of growing inequality.

Before the invention of signs to represent riches, wealth could hardly consist in anything but lands and cattle, the only real possessions men can have. But, when inheritances so increased in number and extent as to occupy the whole of the land, and to border on one another, one man could aggrandize himself only at the expense of another; at the same time the supernumeraries, who had been too weak or too indolent to make such acquisitions, and had grown poor without sustaining any loss, because while they saw everything change around them, they remained still the same, were obliged to receive their subsistence, or steal it, from the rich; and this soon bred, according to their different characters, dominion and slavery, or violence and rapine. The wealthy, on their part, had no sooner begun to taste the pleasure of command, than they disdained all others, and, using their old slaves to acquire new, thought of nothing but subduing and enslaving their neighbours; like ravenous wolves, which, having once tasted human flesh, despise every other food and thenceforth seek only men to devour. . . .

In these different governments,* all the offices were at first elective; and when the influence of wealth was out of the question, the preference was given to merit, which gives a natural ascendancy, and to age, which is experienced in business and deliberate in council. The Elders of the Hebrews, the Gerontes at Sparta, the Senate at Rome, and the very etymology of our word Seigneur, show how old age was once held in veneration. But the more often the choice fell upon old men, the more often elections had to be repeated, and the more they became a nuisance; intrigues set in, factions were formed, party feeling grew bitter, civil wars broke out; the lives of individuals were sacrificed to the pretended happiness of the State; and at length men were on the point of relapsing into their primitive anarchy. Ambitious chiefs profited by these circumstances to perpetuate their offices in their own families: at the same time the people, already used to dependence, ease, and the conveniences of life, and already incapable of breaking its fetters, agreed to an increase of its slavery, in order to secure its tranquillity. Thus magistrates, having become hereditary, contracted the habit of considering their offices as a family estate, and themselves as proprietors

* These refer to examples which have been omitted for the sake of brevity.

of the communities of which they were at first only the officers, of regarding their fellow-citizens as their slaves, and numbering them, like cattle, among their belongings, and of calling themselves the equals of the gods and kings of kings.

If we follow the progress of inequality in these various revolutions,* we shall find that the establishment of laws and of the right of property was its first term, the institution of magistracy the second, and the conversion of legitimate into arbitrary power the third and last; so that the condition of rich and poor was authorized by the first period; that of powerful and weak by the second; and only by the third that of master and slave, which is the last degree of inequality, and the term at which all the rest remain, when they have got so far, till the government is either entirely dissolved by new revolutions, or brought back again to legitimacy.

To understand this progress as necessary we must consider not so much the motives for the establishment of the body politic, as the forms it assumes in actuality, and the faults that necessarily attend it: for the flaws which make social institutions necessary are the same as make the abuse of them unavoidable. If we except Sparta, where the laws were mainly concerned with the education of children, and where Lycurgus established such morality as practically made laws needless — for laws as a rule, being weaker than the passions, restrain men without altering them — it would not be difficult to prove that every government, which scrupulously complied with the ends for which it was instituted, and guarded carefully against change and corruption, was set up unnecessarily. For a country, in which no one either evaded the laws or made a bad use of magisterial power, could require neither laws nor magistrates.

Political distinctions necessarily produce civil distinctions. The growing equality between the chiefs and the people is soon felt by individuals, and modified in a thousand ways according to passions, talents, and circumstances. The magistrate could not usurp any illegitimate power, without giving distinction to the creatures with whom he must share it. Besides, individuals only allow themselves to be oppressed so far as they are hurried on by blind ambition, and, looking rather below than above them, come to love authority more than independence, and submit to slavery, that they may in turn enslave others. It is no easy matter to reduce to obedience a man who has no ambition to command; nor would the most adroit politician find it possible to enslave a people whose only desire was to be independent. But inequality easily makes its way among cowardly and ambitious minds, which are ever ready to run the risks of fortune, and almost indifferent whether they command or obey, as it is favourable or

---

* By revolutions Rousseau, like other writers of the time, means changes (ed.).

adverse. Thus, there must have been a time, when the eyes of the people were so fascinated, that their rulers had only to say to the least of men, 'Be great, you and all your posterity,' to make him immediately appear great in the eyes of every one as well as in his own. His descendants took still more upon them, in proportion to their distance from him; the more obscure and uncertain the cause, the greater the effect: the greater the number of idlers one could count in a family, the more illustrious it was held to be.

If this were the place to go into details, I could readily explain how, even without the intervention of government, inequality of credit and authority became unavoidable among private persons, as soon as their union in a single society made them compare themselves one with another, and take into account the differences which they found out from the continual intercourse every man had to have with his neighbours. These differences are of several kinds; but riches, nobility or rank, power and personal merit being the principal distinctions by which men form an estimate of each other in society, I could prove that the harmony or conflict of these different forces is the surest indication of the good or bad constitution of a State. I could show that among these four kinds of inequality, personal qualities being the origin of all the others, wealth is the one to which they are all reduced in the end; for, as riches tend most immediately to the prosperity of individuals, and are easiest to communicate, they are used to purchase every other distinction. By this observation we are enabled to judge pretty exactly how far a people has departed from its primitive constitution, and of its progress towards the extreme term of corruption. I could explain how much this universal desire for reputation, honours, and advancement, which inflames us all, exercises and holds up to comparison our faculties and powers; how it excites and multiplies our passions, and, by creating universal competition and rivalry, or rather enmity, among men, occasions numberless failures, successes, and disturbances of all kinds by making so many aspirants run the same course. I could show that it is to this desire of being talked about, and this unremitting rage of distinguishing ourselves, that we owe the best and the worst things we possess, both our virtues and our vices, our science and our errors, our conquerors and our philosophers; that is to say, a great many bad things, and a very few good ones. In a word, I could prove that, if we have a few rich and powerful men on the pinnacle of fortune and grandeur, while the crowd grovels in want and obscurity, it is because the former prize what they enjoy only in so far as others are destitute of it; and because, without changing their condition, they would cease to be happy the moment the people ceased to be wretched.

These details alone, however, would furnish matter for a considerable work, in which the advantages and disadvantages of every kind of government might be weighed, as they are related to man in the state of nature, and at the same time all the different aspects, under which inequality has up to the present appeared, or may appear in ages yet to come, according to the nature of the several governments, and the alterations which time must unavoidably occasion in them, might be demonstrated. We should then see the multitude oppressed from within, in consequence of the very precautions it had taken to guard against foreign tyranny. We should see oppression continually gain ground without its being possible for the oppressed to know where it would stop, or what legitimate means was left them of checking its progress. We should see the rights of citizens and the freedom of nations slowly extinguished, and the complaints, protests, and appeals of the weak treated as seditious murmurings. We should see the honour of defending the common cause confined by statecraft to a mercenary part of the people. We should see taxes made necessary by such means, and the disheartened husbandman deserting his fields even in the midst of peace, and leaving the plough to gird on the sword. We should see fatal and capricious codes of honour established; and the champions of their country sooner or later becoming its enemies, and for ever holding their daggers to the breasts of their fellow-citizens. ...

From great inequality of fortunes and conditions, from the vast variety of passions and of talents, of useless and pernicious arts, of vain sciences, would arise a multitude of prejudices equally contrary to reason, happiness, and virtue. We should see the magistrates fomenting everything that might weaken men united in society, by promoting dissension among them; everything that might sow in it the seeds of actual division, while it gave society the air of harmony; everything that might inspire the different ranks of people with mutual hatred and distrust, by setting the rights and interests of one against those of another, and so strengthen the power which comprehended them all.

It is from the midst of this disorder and these revolutions, that despotism, gradually raising up its hideous head and devouring everything that remained sound and untainted in any part of the State, would at length trample on both the laws and the people, and establish itself on the ruins of the republic. The times which immediately preceded this last change would be times of trouble and calamity; but at length the monster would swallow up everything, and the people would no longer have either chiefs or laws, but only tyrants. From this moment there would be no question of virtue or morality; for despotism *(cui ex honesto nulla est spes),* wherever it prevails, admits no other master; it no sooner speaks than probity and duty lose their weight and blind obedience is the only virtue which slaves can still practise. ...

The savage and the civilized man differ so much in the bottom of their hearts and in their inclinations, that what constitutes the supreme happiness of one would reduce the other to despair. The former breathes only peace and liberty; he desires only to live and be free from labour; even the *ataraxia* of the Stoic falls far short of his profound indifference to every other object. Civilized man, on the other hand, is always moving, sweating, toiling, and racking his brains to find still more laborious occupations: he goes on in drudgery to his last moment, and even seeks death to put himself in a position to live, or renounces life to acquire immortality. He pays his court to men in power, whom he hates, and to the wealthy, whom he despises; he stops at nothing to have the honour of serving them; he is not ashamed to value himself on his own meanness and their protection; and, proud of his slavery, he speaks with disdain of those, who have not the honour of sharing it. What a sight would the perplexing and envied labours of a European minister of State present to the eyes of a Caribbean! How many cruel deaths would not this indolent savage prefer to the horrors of such a life, which is seldom even sweetened by the pleasure of doing good! But, for him to see into the motives of all this solicitude the words 'power' and 'reputation' would have to bear some meaning in his mind; he would have to know that there are men who set a value on the opinion of the rest of the world; who can be made happy and satisfied with themselves rather on the testimony of other people than on their own. In reality, the source of all these differences is, that the savage lives within himself, while social man lives constantly outside himself, and only knows how to live in the opinion of others, so that he seems to receive the consciousness of his own existence merely from the judgment of others concerning him. It is not to my present purpose to insist on the indifference to good and evil which arises from this disposition, in spite of our many fine works on morality, or to show how, everything being reduced to appearances, there is but art and mummery in even honour, friendship, virtue, and often vice itself, of which we at length learn the secret of boasting; to show, in short, how, always asking others what we are, and never daring to ask ourselves, in the midst of so much philosophy, humanity, and civilization, and of such sublime codes of morality, we have nothing to show for ourselves but a frivolous and deceitful appearance, honour without virtue, reason without wisdom, and pleasure without happiness. It is sufficient that I have proved that this is not by any means the original state of man, but that it is merely the spirit of society, and the inequality which society produces, that thus transform and alter all our natural inclinations.

    I have endeavoured to trace the origin and progress of inequality, and the institution and abuse of political societies, as far as these are capable of being deduced from the nature of man merely by the light of reason, and independently of those sacred dogmas which give the sanction of divine right to sovereign authority. It follows from this survey that, as there is hardly any inequality in the state of nature, all the inequality which now prevails owes its strength and growth to the development of our faculties and the advance of the human mind, and becomes at last permanent and legitimate by the establishment of property and laws. Secondly, it follows that moral inequality, authorized by positive right alone, clashes with natural right, whenever it is not proportionate to physical inequality — a distinction which sufficiently determines what we ought to think of that species of inequality which prevails in all civilized countries; since it is plainly contrary to the law of nature, however defined, that children should command old men, fools wise men, and that the privileged few should gorge themselves with superfluities, while the starving multitude are in want of the bare necessities of life.

Source: from *The Social Contract and Discourses,* trans. G.D.H. Cole (Everyman edn., J.M. Dent, London, 1966) pp. 193-203, 214-21.

7 CIVIL GOVERNMENT IS FOR DEFENCE OF RICH AGAINST POOR*

Adam Smith

Among nations of hunters, as there is scarce any property, or at least none that exceeds the value of two or three days' labour, so there is seldom any established magistrate or any regular administration of justice. Men who have no property can injure one another only in their persons or reputations. But when one man kills, wounds, beats, or defames another, though he to whom the injury is done suffers, he who does it receives no benefit. It is otherwise with the injuries to property. The benefit of the person who does the injury is often equal to the loss of him who suffers it. Envy, malice, or resentment, are the only passions which can prompt one man to injure another in his person or reputation. But the greater part of men are not very frequently under the influence of those passions, and the very worst men are so only occasionally. As their gratification, too, how aggreable soever it may be to certain characters, is not attended with any real or permanent advantage, it is in greater part of men commonly restrained by prudential considerations. Men may live together in society with some tolerable degree of security, though there is no civil magistrate to protect them from the injustice of those passions. But avarice and ambition in the rich, in the poor the hatred of labour and the love of present ease and enjoyment, are the passions which prompt to invade property; passions much more steady in their operation, and much more universal in their influence. Wherever there is great property, there is great inequality. For one very rich man, there must be at least five hundred poor, and the affluence of the rich excites the indignation of the poor, who are often both driven by want and prompted by envy to invade his possessions. It is only under the shelter of the civil magistrate that the owner of that valuable property, which is acquired by the labour of many years, or perhaps of many successive generations, can sleep a single night in security. He is at all times surrounded by unknown enemies, whom, though he never provoked, he can never appease, and from whose injustice he can be protected only by the powerful arm of the civil magistrate continually held up to chastise it. The acquisition of valuable and extensive property, therefore, necessarily requires the establishment of civil government. Where there is no property, or at least none that exceeds

---

* This is Smith's own page heading.

the value of two or three days' labour, civil government is not so necessary.

Civil government supposes a certain subordination. But as the necessity of civil government gradually grows up with the acquisition of valuable property, so the principal causes which naturally introduce subordination gradually grow up with the growth of that valuable property. The cause of circumstances which naturally introduce subordination or which naturally, and antecedent to any civil institution, give some men some superiority over the greater part of their brethren, seem to be four in number.

The first of those causes or circumstances is the superiority of personal qualifications — of strength, beauty, and agility of body; of wisdom and virtue, of prudence, justice, fortitude, and moderation of mind. The qualifications of the body, unless supported by those of the mind, can give little authority in any period of society. He is a very strong man who, by mere strength of body, can force two weak ones to obey him. The qualifications of the mind can alone give very great authority. They are, however, invisible qualities; always disputable, and generally disputed. No society, whether barbarous or civilized, has ever found it convenient to settle the rules of precedency of rank and subordination according to those invisible qualities, but according to something that is more plain and palpable.

The second of those causes or circumstances is the superiority of age. An old man, provided his age is not so far advanced as to give suspicion of dotage, is everywhere more respected than a young man of equal rank, fortune, and abilities. Among nations of hunters, such as the native tribes of North America, age is the sole foundation of rank and precedency. Among them, father is the appellation of a superior; brother, of an equal; and son, of an inferior. In the most opulent and civilized nations, age regulates rank among those who are in every other respect equal, and among whom, therefore, there is nothing else to regulate it. Among brothers and among sisters the eldest always takes place; and in the succession of the paternal estate, everything which cannot be divided, but must go entire to one person, such as a title of honour, is in most cases given to the eldest. Age is a plain and palpable quality which admits of no dispute.

The third of those causes or circumstances is the superiority of fortune. The authority of riches, however, though great in every age of society, is perhaps greatest in the rudest age of society which admits of any considerable inequality of fortune. A Tartar chief, the increase of whose herds and flocks is sufficient to maintain a thousand men, cannot well employ that increase in any other way than in maintaining a thousand men. The rude state of his society does not afford him any manufactured produce, any trinkets or baubles of any kind, for which he can exchange that part of his rude produce which is over and above his own consumption. The 1,000 men whom he thus maintains, depending entirely upon him for their subsistence, must both obey his orders in war and submit to his jurisdiction in peace. He is necessarily both their general and their judge, and his chieftainship is the necessary effect of the superiority of his fortune. In an opulent and civilized society, a man may possess a much greater fortune, and yet not be able to command a dozen of people. Though the produce of his estate may be sufficient to maintain, and may perhaps actually maintain, more than 1,000 people, yet as those people pay for everything which they get from him, as he gives scarce anything to anybody but in exchange for an equivalent, there is scarce anybody who considers himself as entirely dependent upon him, and his authority extends only over a few menial servants. The authority of fortune, however, is very great even in an opulent and civilized society. That it is much greater than that, either of age, or of personal qualities, has been the constant complaint of every period of society which admitted of any considerable inequality of fortune. The first period of society, that of hunters, admits of no such inequality. Universal poverty establishes their universal equality, and the superiority either of age or of personal qualities, are the feeble, but the sole foundations of authority and subordination. There is therefore little or no authority or subordination in this period of society. The second period of society, that of shepherds, admits of very great inequalities of fortune, and there is no period in which the superiority of fortune gives so great authority to those who possess it. There is no period accordingly in which authority and subordination are more perfectly established. The authority of an Arabian scherif is very great; that of a Tartar khan altogether despotical.

The fourth of those causes or circumstances is the superiority of birth. Superiority of birth supposes an ancient superiority of fortune in the family of the person who claims it. All families are equally ancient; and the ancestors of the prince, though they may be better known, cannot well be more numerous than those of the beggar. Antiquity of family means everywhere the antiquity either founded upon wealth or accompanied with it. Upstart greatness is everywhere less respected than ancient greatness. The hatred of usurpers, the love of the family of an ancient monarch, are, in a great measure, founded upon the contempt which men naturally have for the former, and upon their veneration for the latter. As a military officer submits without reluctance to the authority of a superior by whom he has always been commanded, but cannot bear that his inferior should be set over his head, so men easily submit to a family to whom they and their ancestors have always submitted; but are fired with indignation when another family, in whom they had never acknowledged any such superiority, assumes a dominion over them.

The distinction of birth, being subsequent to the inequality of fortune, can have no place in nations of hunters, among whom all men, being equal in fortune, must likewise be very nearly equal in birth. The son of a wise and brave man may, indeed, even among them, be somewhat more respected than a man of equal merit who has the misfortune to be the son of a fool or a coward. The difference, however, will not be very great; and there never was, I believe, a great family in the world whose illustration was entirely derived from the inheritance of wisdom and virtue.

The distinction of birth not only may, but always does, take place among nations of shepherds. Such nations are always strangers to every sort of luxury, and great wealth can scarce ever be dissipated among them by improvident profusion. There are no nations accordingly who abound more in families revered and honoured on account of their descent from a long race of great and illustrious ancestors; because there are no nations among whom wealth is likely to continue longer in the same families.

Birth and fortune are evidently the two circumstances which principally set one man above another. They are the two great sources of personal distinction, and are therefore the principal causes which naturally establish authority and subordination among men. Among nations of shepherds both these causes operate with their full force. The great shepherd or herdsman, respected on account of his great wealth, and of the great number of those who depend upon him for subsistence, and revered on account of the nobleness of his birth and of the immemorial antiquity of his illustrious family, has a natural authority over all the inferior shepherds or herdsmen of his horde or clan. He can command the united force of a greater number of people than any of them. His military power is greater than that of any of them. In time of war they are all of them naturally disposed to muster themselves under his banner, rather than under that of any other person, and his birth and fortune thus naturally procure to him some sort of executive power. By commanding, too, the united force of a greater number of people than any of them, he is best able to compel any one of them who may have injured another to compensate the wrong. He is the person, therefore, to whom all those who are too weak to defend themselves naturally look up for protection. It is to him that they naturally complain of the injuries which they imagine have been done to them, and his interposition in such cases is more easily submitted to, even by the persons complained of, than that of any other person would be. His birth and fortune thus naturally procure him some sort of judicial authority.

It is in the age of shepherds, in the second period of society, that the inequality of fortune first begins to take place, and introduces among men a degree of authority and subordination which could not possibly exist before. It thereby introduces some degree of that civil government which is indispensably necessary for its own preservation: and it seems to do this naturally, and ever dependent of the consideration of that necessity. The consideration of that necessity comes, no doubt, afterwards to contribute very much to maintain and secure that authority and subordination. The rich, in particular, are necessarily interested to support that order of things, which can alone secure them in the possession of their own advantages. Men of inferior wealth combine to defend those of superior wealth in the possession of their property, in order that men of superior wealth may combine to defend them in the possession of theirs. All the inferior shepherds and herdsmen feel that the security of their own herds and flocks depends upon the security of those of the great shepherd or herdsman; and the maintenance of their lesser authority depends upon that of his greater authority, and that upon their subordination depends his power of keeping their inferiors in subordination to them. They constitute a sort of little nobility, who feel themselves interested to defend the property and to support the authority of their own little sovereign, in order that he may be able to defend their property and to support their authority. Civil government, so far as it is instituted for the security of property, is in reality instituted for the defence of the rich against the poor, or of those who have some property against those who have none at all. . . .

Very old families, such as have possessed some considerable estate from father to son for many successive generations, are very rare in commercial countries. In countries which have little commerce, on the contrary, such as Wales or the Highlands of Scotland, they are very common. The Arabian histories seem to be all full of genealogies, and there is a history written by a Tartar Khan, which has been translated into several European languages, and which contains scarce anything else; a proof that ancient families are very common among those nations. In countries where a rich man can spend his revenue in no other way than by maintaining as many people as it can maintain, he is not apt to run out, and his benevolence it seems is seldom so violent as to attempt to maintain more than he can afford. But where he can spend the greatest revenue upon his own person, he frequently has no bounds to his expense, because he frequently has no bounds to his vanity, or to his affection for his own person. In commercial countries, therefore, riches, in spite of the most violent regulations of law to prevent their dissipation, very seldom remain long in the same family. Among simple nations, on the contrary, they frequently do without any regulations of law; for among nations of shepherds, such as the Tartars and Arabs, the consumable nature of their property necessarily renders all such regulations impossible.

A revolution of the greatest importance to the public happiness, was in this manner brought about by two different orders of people, who had not the least intention to serve the public. To gratify the most childish vanity was the sole motive of the great proprietors. The merchants and artificers, much less ridiculous, acted merely from a view to their own interest, and in pursuit of their own pedlar principle of turning a penny wherever a penny was to be got. Neither of them had knowledge or foresight of that great revolution which the folly of the one, and industry of the other, was gradually bringing about.

Source: from *An Inquiry into the Nature and Causes of the Wealth of Nations* (Routledge & Sons, London,) pp. 556-60, 318-19.

8 OF THE ORIGIN OF AMBITION AND OF THE DISTINCTION OF RANKS

Adam Smith

It is because mankind are disposed to sympathize more entirely with our joy than with our sorrow, that we make parade of our riches and conceal our poverty. Nothing is so mortifying as to be obliged to expose our distress to the view of the public and feel that, though our situation is open to the eyes of all mankind, no mortal conceives for us the half of what we suffer. Nay, it is chiefly from this regard to the sentiments of mankind that we pursue riches and avoid poverty. For to what purpose is all the toil and bustle of this world? What is the end of avarice and ambition, of the pursuit of wealth, of power, and preeminence? Is it to supply the necessities of nature? The wages of the meanest labourer can supply them. We see that they afford him food and clothing, the comfort of a house and of a family. If we examine his economy with rigor, we should find that he spends a great part of them upon conveniences which may be regarded as superfluities, and that, upon extraordinary occasions, he can give something even to vanity and distinction. What then is the cause of our aversion to his situation, and why should those who have been educated in the higher ranks of life regard it as worse than death to be reduced to live, even without labour, upon the same simple fare with him, to dwell under the same lowly roof, and to be clothed in the same humble attire? Do they imagine that their stomach is better or their sleep sounder in a palace than in a cottage? The contrary has been so often observed, . . . that there is nobody ignorant of it. From whence, then, arises that emulation which runs through all the different ranks of men, and what are the advantages which we propose by that great purpose of human life which we call bettering our condition? To be observed, to be attended to, to be taken notice of with sympathy, complacency, and approbation, are all the advantages which we can propose to derive from it. It is the vanity, not the ease or the pleasure, which interests us. But vanity is always founded upon the belief of our being the object of attention and approbation. The rich man glories in his riches, because he feels that they naturally draw upon him the attention of the world, and that mankind are disposed to go along with him in all those agreeable emotions with which the advantages of his situation so readily inspire him. At the thought of this, his heart seems to swell and dilate itself within him, and he is fonder of his wealth, upon this account, than for all the other advantages it procures him. The poor man, on the contrary, is ashamed of his poverty. He feels that it either places him out of the sight of mankind, or that, if they take any notice of him, they have, however, scarce any fellow-feeling with the misery and distress which he suffers. He is mortified upon both accounts; for though to be overlooked and to be disapproved of are things entirely different, yet, as obscurity covers us from the daylight of honour and approbation, to feel that we are taken no notice of necessarily damps the most agreeable hope and disappoints the most ardent desire of human nature. The poor man goes out and comes in unheeded, and, when in the midst of a crowd, is in the same obscurity as if shut up in his own hovel. Those humble cares and painful attentions which occupy those in his situation afford no amusement to the dissipated and the gay. They turn away their eyes from him or, if the extremity of his distress forces them to look at him, it is only to spurn so disagreeable an object from among them. The fortunate and the proud wonder at the insolence of human wretchedness, that it should dare to present itself before them and with the loathsome aspect of its misery presume to disturb the serenity of their happiness. The man of rank and distinction, on the contrary, is observed by all the world. Everybody is eager to look at him and to conceive, at least by sympathy, that joy and exultation with which his circumstances naturally inspire him. His actions are the objects of the public care. Scarce a word, scarce a gesture, can fall from him that is altogether neglected. In a great assembly he is the person upon whom all direct their eyes; it is upon him that their passions seem all to wait with expectation, in order to receive that movement and direction which he shall impress upon them; and if his behaviour is not altogether absurd, he has, every moment, an opportunity of interesting mankind, and of rendering himself the object of the observation and fellow-feeling of everybody about him. It is this which, notwithstanding the restraint it imposes, notwithstanding the loss of liberty with which it is attended, renders greatness the object of envy, and compensates, in the opinion of mankind, all that toil, all that anxiety, all those mortifications, which must be undergone in the pursuit of it, and, what is of yet more consequence, all that leisure, all that ease, all that careless security, which are forfeited forever by the acquisition.

    When we consider the condition of the great in those delusive colours in which the imagination is apt to paint it, it seems to be almost the abstract idea of a perfect and happy state. It is the very state which, in all our waking dreams and idle reveries, we had sketched out to ourselves as the final object of all our desires. We feel, therefore, a peculiar sympathy with the satisfaction of those who are in it. We favour all their inclinations and forward all their wishes. What pity, we think, that anything should spoil and corrupt so agreeable a situation! We could even wish them immortal; and it seems hard to us that death should at last put an end to such perfect enjoyment. It is cruel, we think, in nature to compel them from their exalted stations to that humble, but hospitable, home, which she has provided for all her children. Great king, live for ever! is the compliment which, after the manner of eastern adulation, we should readily make them if experience did not teach us its absurdity. Every calamity that befalls them, every injury that is done them, excites in the breast of the spectator ten times more compassion and resentment than he would have felt had the same things happened to other men. It is the misfortunes of kings only which afford the proper subjects for tragedy. They resemble, in this respect, the misfortunes of lovers. Those two situations are the chief which interest us upon the theatre, because, in spite of all that reason and experience can tell us to the contrary, the prejudices of the imagination attach to these two states a happiness superior to any other. To disturb or to put an end to such perfect enjoyment seems to be the most atrocious of all injuries. The traitor who conspires against the life of his monarch is thought a greater monster than any other murderer. All the innocent blood that was shed in the civil wars provoked less indignation than the death of Charles I. A stranger to human nature, who saw the indifference of men about the misery of their inferiors and the regret and indignation which they feel for the misfortunes and sufferings of those above them, would be apt to imagine that pain must be more agonizing and the convulsions of death more terrible to persons of higher rank than to those of meaner stations.

Upon this disposition of mankind to go along with all the passions of the rich and the powerful is founded the distinction of ranks and the order of society. Our obsequiousness to our superiors more frequently arises from our admiration for the advantages of their situation than from any private expectations of benefit from thier good-will. Their benefits can extend but to a few, but their fortunes interest almost everybody. We are eager to assist them in completing a system of happiness that approaches so near to perfection; and we desire to serve them for their own sake, without any other recompense but vanity or the honour of obliging them. Neither is our deference to their inclinations founded chiefly, or altogether, upon a regard to the utility of such submission, and to the order of society which is best supported by it. Even when the order of society seems to require that we should oppose them, we can hardly bring ourselves to do it. That kings are the servants of the people, to be obeyed, resisted, deposed, or punished, as the public convenience may require, is the doctrine of reason and philosophy; but it is not the doctrine of nature. Nature would teach us to submit to them for their own sake, to tremble and bow down before their exalted station, to regard their smile as a reward sufficient to compensate any services, and to dread their displeasure, though no other evil were to follow from it, as the severest of all mortifications. To treat them in any respect as men, to reason and dispute with them upon ordinary occasions, requires such resolution that there are few men whose magnanimity can support them in it, unless they are likewise assisted by familiarity and acquaintance. The strongest motives, the most furious passions, fear, hatred, and resentment, are scarce sufficient to balance this natural disposition to respect them; and their conduct must, either justly or unjustly, have excited the highest degree of all those passions, before the bulk of the people can be brought to oppose them with violence or to desire to see them either punished or deposed. Even when the people have been brought this length, they are apt to relent every moment, and easily relapse into their habitual state of deference to those to whom they have been accustomed to look up to as their natural superiors. They cannot stand the mortification of their monarch. Compassion soon takes the place of resentment, they forget all past provocations, their old principles of loyalty revive, and they run to re-establish the ruined authority of their old masters with the same violence with which they had opposed it. The death of Charles I brought about the restoration of the royal family. Compassion for James II, when he was seized by the populace in making his escape on ship-board, had almost prevented the revolution, and made it go on more heavily than before.

    Do the great seem insensible of the easy price at which they may acquire the public admiration, or do they seem to imagine that to them, as to other men, it must be the purchase either of sweat or of blood? By what important accomplishments is the young nobleman instructed to support the dignity of his rank, and to render himself worthy of that superiority over his fellow citizens, to which the virtue of his ancestors had raised them? Is it by knowledge, by industry, by patience, by self-denial, or by virtue of any kind? As all his words, as all his motions are attended to, he learns an habitual regard to every circumstance of ordinary behaviour, and studies to perform all those small duties with the most exact propriety. As he is conscious how much he is observed, and how much mankind are disposed to favour all his inclinations, he acts, upon the most indifferent occasions, with that freedom and elevation which the thought of this naturally inspires. His air, his manner, his deportment, all mark that elegant and graceful sense of his own superiority, which those who are born to inferior stations can hardly ever arrive at. These are the arts by which he proposes to make mankind more easily submit to his authority and to govern their inclinations according to his own pleasure; and in this he is seldom disappointed. These arts, supported by rank and pre-eminence, are, upon ordinary occasions, sufficient to govern the world. Louis XIV, during the greater part of his reign, was regarded not only in France, but over all Europe, as the most perfect model of a great prince. But what were the talents and virtues by which he acquired this great reputation? Was it by the scrupulous and inflexible justice of all his undertakings, by the immense dangers and difficulties with which they were attended, or by the unwearied and unrelenting application with which he pursued them? Was it by his extensive knowledge, by his exquisite judgment, or by his heroic valour? It was by none of these qualities. But he was, first of all, the most powerful prince in Europe, and consequently held the highest rank among kings; and then, says his historian:

He surpassed all his courtiers in the gracefulness of his shape and the majestic beauty of his features. The sound of his voice, noble and affecting, gained those hearts which his presence intimidated. He had a step and a deportment which could suit only him and his rank, and which would have been ridiculous in any other person. The embarrassment which he occasioned to those who spoke to him flattered that secret satisfaction with which he felt his own superiority. The old officer, who was confounded and faltered in asking him a favour, and not being able to conclude his discourse, said to him: 'Sir, your majesty, I hope, will believe that I do not tremble thus before your enemies,' had no difficulty to obtain what he demanded. These frivolous accomplishments, supported by his rank and, no doubt too, by a degree of other talents and virtues which seem, however, not to have been much above mediocrity, established this prince in the esteem of his own age, and have drawn even from posterity a good deal of respect for his memory. Compared with these, in his own times and in his own presence, no other virtue, it seems, appeared to have any merit. Knowledge, industry, valour, and beneficence trembled, were abashed, and lost all dignity before them.

But it is not by accomplishments of this kind that the man of inferior rank must hope to distinguish himself. Politeness is so much the virtue of the great that it will do little honour to anybody but themselves. The coxcomb, who imitates their manner and affects to be eminent by the superior propriety of his ordinary behaviour, is rewarded with a double share of contempt for his folly and presumption. Why should the man whom nobody thinks it worth while to look at be very anxious about the manner in which he holds up his head, or disposes of his arms, while he walks through a room? He is occupied surely with a very superfluous attention, and with an attention, too, that marks a sense of his own importance which no other mortal can go along with. The most perfect modesty and plainness, joined to as much negligence as is consistent with the respect due to the company, ought to be the chief characteristics of the behaviour of a private man. If ever he hopes to distinguish himself, it must be more important virtues. He must acquire dependents to balance the dependents of the great, and he has no other fund to pay them from but the labour of his body and the activity of his mind. He must cultivate these therefore; he must acquire superior knowledge in his profession, and superior industry in the exercise of it. He must be patient in labour, resolute in danger, and firm in distress. These talents he must bring into public view, by the difficulty, importance, and, at the same time, good judgment of his undertakings, and by the severe and unrelenting application with which he pursues them. Probity and prudence, generosity and frankness, must characterize his behaviour upon all ordinary occasions; and he must, at the same time, be forward to engage in all those situations in which it requires the greatest talents and virtues to act with propriety, but in which the greatest applause is to be acquired by those who can acquit themselves with honour. With what impatience does the man of spirit and ambition, who is depressed by his situation, look round for some great opportunity to distinguish himself? No circumstances which can afford this appear to him undesirable. He even looks forward with satisfaction to the prospect of foreign war or civil dissension, and, with secret transport and delight, sees through all the confusion and bloodshed which attend them the probability of those wished-for occasions presenting themselves, in which he may draw upon himself the attention and admiration of mankind. The man of rank and distinction, on the contrary, whose whole glory consists in the propriety of his ordinary behaviour, who is contented with the humble renown which this can afford him and has no talents to acquire any other, is unwilling to embarrass himself with what can be attended either with difficulty or distress. To figure at a ball is his great triumph, and to succeed in an intrigue of gallantry his highest exploit. He has an aversion to all public confusions, not from the love of mankind — for the great never look upon their inferiors as their fellow creatures — nor yet from want of courage — for in that he is seldom defective — but from a consciousness that he possesses none of the virtues which are required in such situations, and that the public attention will certainly be drawn away from him by others. He may be willing to expose himself to some little danger and to make a campaign when it happens to be the fashion, but he shudders with horror at the thought of any situation which demands the continual and long exertion of patience, industry, fortitude, and application of thought. These virtues are hardly ever to be met with in men who are born to those high stations. In all governments accordingly, even in monarchies, the highest offices are generally possessed, and the whole detail of the administration conducted, by men who were educated in the middle and inferior ranks of life, who have been carried forward by their own industry and abilities, though loaded with the jealousy and opposed by the resentment of all those who were born their superiors, and to whom the great, after having regarded them first with contempt and afterwards with envy, are at last contented to truckle with the same abject meanness with which they desire that the rest of mankind should behave to themselves.

It is the loss of this easy empire over the affections of mankind which renders the fall from greatness so insupportable. When the family of the king of Macedon was led in triumph by Paulus Emilius, their misfortunes, it is said, made them divide with their conqueror the attention of the Roman people. The sight of the royal children, whose tender age rendered them insensible of their situation, struck the spectators, amidst the public rejoicings and prosperity, with the tenderest sorrow and compassion. The king appeared next in the procession and seemed like one confounded and astonished, and bereft of all sentiment, by the greatness of his calamities. His friends and ministers followed after him. As they moved along, they often cast their eyes upon their fallen sovereign and always burst into tears at the sight, their whole behaviour demonstrating that they thought not of their own misfortunes, but were occupied entirely by the superior greatness of his. The generous Romans, on the contrary, beheld him with disdain and indignation, and regarded as unworthy of all compassion the man who could be so mean-spirited as to bear to live under such calamities. Yet what did those calamities amount to? According to the greater part of historians he was to spend the remainder of his days under the protection of a powerful and humane people, in a state which in itself should seem worthy of envy, a state of plenty, ease, leisure, and security, from which it was impossible for him, even by his own folly, to fall. But he was no longer to be surrounded by that admiring mob of fools, flatterers, and dependents, who had formerly been accustomed to attend upon all his motions. He was no longer to be gazed upon by multitudes, nor to have it in his power to render himself the object of their respect, their gratitude, their love, their admiration. The passions of nations were no longer to mould themselves upon his inclinations. This was that insupportable calamity which bereaved the king of all sentiment, which made his friends forget their own misfortunes, and which the Roman magnanimity could scarce conceive how any man could be so mean-spirited as to bear to survive.

'Love', says my Lord Rochefoucauld, 'is commonly succeeded by ambition, but ambition is hardly ever succeeded by love.' That passion, when once it has got entire possession of the breast, will admit neither a rival nor a successor. To those who have been accustomed to the possession, or even to the hope, of public admiration, all other pleasures sicken and decay. Of all the discarded statesmen who, for their own ease, have studied to get the better of ambition, and to despise those honours which they could no longer arrive at, how few have been able to succeed? The greater part have spent their time in the most listless and insipid indolence, chagrined at the thoughts of their own insignificance, incapable of being interested in the occupations of private life, without enjoyment except when they talked of their former greatness, and without satisfaction except when they were employed in some vain project to recover it. Are you in earnest resolved never to barter your liberty for the lordly servitude of a court, but to live free, fearless, and independent? There seems to be one way to continue in that virtuous resolution, and perhaps but one. Never enter the place from whence so few have been able to return, never come within the circle of ambition, nor ever bring yourself into comparison with those masters of the earth who have already engrossed the attention of half mankind before you.

Of such mighty importance does it appear to be, in the imaginations of men, to stand in that situation which sets them most in the view of general sympathy and attention. And thus *Place,* that great object which divides the wives of aldermen, is the end of half the labours of human life, and is the cause of all the tumult and bustle, all the rapine and injustice, which avarice and ambition have introduced into this world. People of sense, it is said, indeed despise 'place'; that is, they despise sitting at the head of the table, and are indifferent who it is that is pointed out to the company by that frivolous circumstance, which the smallest advantage is capable of overbalancing. But rank, distinction, pre-eminence, no man despises,unless he is either raised very much above or sunk very much below the ordinary standard of human nature; unless he is either so confirmed in wisdom and real philosophy as to be satisfied that, while the propriety of his conduct renders him the just object of approbation, it is of little consequence though he be neither attended to nor approved of; or so habituated to the idea of his own meanness, so sunk in slothful and sottish indifference, as entirely to have forgotten the desire and almost the very wish for superiority.

As to become the natural object of the joyous congratulations and sympathetic attentions of mankind is, in this manner, the circumstance which gives to prosperity all its dazzling splendour; so nothing darkens so much the gloom of adversity as to feel that our misfortunes are the objects, not of the fellow-feeling, but of the contempt and aversion of our brethren. It is upon this account that the most dreadful calamities are not always those which it is most difficult to support. It is often more mortifying to appear in public under small disasters than under great misfortunes. The first excite no sympathy; but the second, though they may excite none that approaches to the anguish of the sufferer, call forth, however, a very lively compassion. The sentiments of the spectators are, in this last case, less wide of those of the sufferer, and their imperfect fellow-feeling lends him some assistance in supporting his misery. Before a gay assembly, a gentleman would be more mortified to appear covered with filth and rags than with blood and wounds. This last situation would interest their pity; the other would provoke their laughter. The judge who orders a criminal to be set in the pillory dishonours him more than if he had condemned him to the scaffold. The great prince who, some years ago, caned a general officer at the head of his army disgraced him irrecoverably. The punishment would have been much less had he shot him through the body. By the laws of honour, to strike with a cane dishonours, to strike with a sword does not, for an obvious reason. Those slighter punishments, when inflicted on a gentleman to whom dishonour is the greatest of all evils, come to be regarded among a humane and generous people as the most dreadful of any. With regard to persons of that rank, therefore, they are universally laid aside; and the law, while it takes their life upon many occasions, respects their honour upon almost all. To scourge a person of quality or to set him in the pillory, upon account of any crime whatever, is a brutality of which no European government except that of Russia is capable.

A brave man is not rendered contemptible by being brought to the scaffold; he is, by being set in the pillory. His behaviour in the one situation may gain him universal esteem and admiration. No behaviour in the other can render him agreeable. The sympathy of the spectators supports him in the one case and saves him from that shame, that consciousness, that his misery is felt by himself only, which is of all sentiments the most insupportable. There is no sympathy in the other, or, if there is any, it is not with his pain, which is a trifle, but with his consciousness of the want of sympathy with which this pain is attended. It is with his shame, not with his sorrow. Those who pity him blush and hang down their heads for him. He droops in the same manner, and feels himself irrecoverably degraded by the punishment, though not by the crime. The man, on the contrary, who dies with resolution, as he is naturally with the erect aspect of esteem and approbation, so he wears himself the same undaunted countenance; and, if the crime does not deprive him of the respect of others, the punishment never will. He has no suspicion that his situation is the object of contempt or derision to anybody, and he can, with propriety, assume the air not only of perfect serenity, but of triumph and exultation.

'Great dangers', says the Cardinal de Retz, 'have their charms, because there is some glory to be got, even when we miscarry. But moderate dangers have nothing but what is horrible, because the loss of reputation always attends the want of success.' His maxim has the same foundation with what we have been just now observing with regard to punishments.

Human virtue is superior to pain, to poverty, to danger, and to death; nor does it even require its utmost efforts to despise them. But to have its misery exposed to insult and derision, to be led in triumph, to be set up for the hand of scorn to point at, is a situation in which its constancy is much more apt to fall. Compared with the contempt of mankind, all other external evils are easily supported.

Of the Corruption of Our Moral Sentiments, Which Is Occasioned by This Disposition to Admire the Rich and the Great, and to Despise or Neglect Persons of Poor and Mean Condition

This disposition to admire, and almost to worship, the rich and the powerful, and to despise or, at least, to neglect persons of poor and mean condition, though necessary both to establish and to maintain the distinction of ranks and the order of society, is, at the same time, the great and most universal cause of the corruption of our moral sentiments. That wealth and greatness are often regarded with the respect and admiration which are due only to wisdom and virtue, and that the contempt, of which vice and folly are the only proper objects, is often most unjustly bestowed upon poverty and weakness, has been the complaint of moralists in all ages.

We desire both to be respectable and to be respected. We dread both to be contemptible and to be contemned. But, upon coming into the world, we soon find that wisdom and virtue are by no means the sole objects of respect, nor vice and folly, of contempt. We frequently see the respectful attentions of the world more strongly directed towards the rich and the great than towards the wise and the virtuous. We see frequently the vices and follies of the powerful much less despised than the poverty and weakness of the innocent. To deserve, to acquire, and to enjoy the respect and admiration of mankind are the great objects of ambition and emulation. Two different roads are presented to us, equally leading to the attainment of this so much desired object; the one, by the study of wisdom and the practice of virtue, the other, by the acquisition of wealth and greatness. Two different characters are presented to our emulation; the one, of proud ambition and ostentatious avidity, the other, of humble modesty and equitable justice. Two different models, two different pictures are held out to us, according to which we may fashion our own character and behaviour; the one more gaudy and glittering in its colouring, the other more correct and more exquisitely beautiful in its outline; the one forcing itself upon the notice of every wandering eye, the other attracting the attention of scarce anybody but the most studious and careful observer. They are the wise and the virtuous chiefly, a select, though, I am afraid, but a small party who are the real and steady admirers of wisdom and virtue. The great mob of mankind are the admirers and worshippers, and, what may seem more extraordinary, most frequently the disinterested admirers and worshippers, of wealth and greatness.

The respect which we feel for wisdom and virtue is, no doubt, different from that which we conceive for wealth and greatness; and it requires no very nice discernment to distinguish the difference. But, notwithstanding this difference, those sentiments bear a very considerable resemblance to one another. In some particular features they are, no doubt, different, but, in the general air of the countenance, they seem to be so very nearly the same that inattentive observers are very apt to mistake the one for the other.

In equal degrees of merit, there is scarce any man who does not respect more the rich and the great than the poor and the humble. With most men the presumption and vanity of the former are much more admired than the real and solid merit of the latter. It is scarce agreeable to good morals, or even to good language, perhaps, to say that mere wealth and greatness, abstracted from merit and virtue, deserve our respect. We must acknowledge, however, that they almost constantly obtain it; and they may, therefore, be considered as, in some respects, the natural objects of it. Those exalted stations may, no doubt, be completely degraded by vice and folly. But the vice and folly must be very great, before they can operate this complete degradation. The profligacy of a man of fashion is looked upon with much less contempt and aversion than that of a man of meaner condition. In the latter, a single transgression of the rules of temperance and propriety is commonly more resented than the constant and avowed contempt of them ever is in the former.

In the middling and inferior stations of life, the road to virtue and that to fortune – to such fortune, at least, as men in such stations can reasonably expect to acquire – are, happily, in most cases very nearly the same. In all the middling and inferior professions, real and solid professional abilities, joined to prudent, just, firm, and temperate conduct, can very seldom fail of success. Abilities will even sometimes prevail where the conduct is by no means correct. Either habitual imprudence, however, or injustice, or weakness, or profligacy, will always cloud, and sometimes depress altogether, the most splendid professional abilities. Men in the inferior and middling stations of life, besides, can never be great enough to be above the law, which must generally overawe them into some sort of respect for at least the more important rules of justice. The success of such people, too, almost always depends upon the favour and good opinion of their neighbours and equals, and without a tolerably regular conduct these can very seldom be obtained. The good old proverb, therefore, that honesty is the best policy, holds, in such situations, almost always perfectly true. In such situations, therefore, we may generally expect a considerable degree of virtue; and, fortunately for the good morals of society, these are the situations of by far the greater part of mankind.

In the superior stations of life the case is unhappily not always the same. In the courts of princes, in the drawing rooms of the great, where success and preferment depend not upon the esteem of intelligent and well informed equals but upon the fanciful and foolish favour of ignorant, presumptuous, and proud superiors, flattery and falsehood too often prevail over merit and abilities. In such societies the abilities to please are more regarded than the abilities to serve. In quiet and peaceable times, when the storm is at a distance, the prince or great man wishes only to be amused, and is even apt to fancy that he has scarce any occasion for the service of anybody, or that those who amuse him are sufficiently able to serve him. The external graces, the frivolous accomplishments of that impertinent and foolish thing called 'a man of fashion' are commonly more admired than the solid and masculine virtues of a warrior, a statesman, a philosopher, or a legislator. All the great and awful virtues, all the virtues which can fit either for the council, the senate, or the field, are by the insolent and insignificant flatterers, who commonly figure the most in such corrupted societies, held in the utmost contempt and derision. When the Duke of Sully was called upon by Louis XIII to give his advice in some great emergency, he observed the favourites and courtiers whispering to one another and smiling at his unfashionable appearance. 'Whenever your majesty's father', said the old warrior and statesman, 'did me the honour to consult me, he ordered the buffoons of the court to retire into the antechamber.'

It is from our disposition to admire and, consequently, to imitate the rich and the great that they are enabled to set or to lead what is called the fashion. Their dress is the fashionable dress, the language of their conversation the fashionable style, their air and deportment the fashionable behaviour. Even their vices and follies are fashionable, and the greater part of men are proud to imitate and resemble them in the very qualities which dishonour and degrade them. Vain men often give themselves airs of a fashionable profligacy which, in their hearts, they do not approve of, and of which, perhaps, they are really not guilty. They desire to be praised for what they themselves do not think praiseworthy, and are ashamed of unfashionable virtues, which they sometimes practise in secret, and for which they have secretly some degree of real veneration. There are hypocrites of wealth and greatness as well as of religion and virtue; and a vain man is as apt to pretend to be what he is not, in the one way, as a cunning man is in the other. He assumes the equipage and splendid way of living of his superiors, without considering that whatever may be praiseworthy in any of these, derives its whole merit and propriety from its suitableness to that situation and fortune, which both require, and can easily support the expense. Many a poor man places his glory in being thought rich, without considering that the duties (if one may call such follies by so very venerable a name) which that reputation imposes upon him must soon reduce him to beggary and render his situation still more unlike that of those whom he admires and imitates than it had been originally.

To attain to this envied situation, the candidates for fortune too frequently abandon the paths of virtue, for, unhappily, the road which leads to the one, and that which leads to the other, lie sometimes in very opposite directions. But the ambitious man flatters himself that, in the splendid situation to which he advances, he will have so many means of commanding the respect and admiration of mankind, and will be enabled to act with such superior propriety and grace, that the lustre of his future conduct will entirely cover, or efface, the foulness of the steps by which he arrived at that elevation. In many governments the candidates for the highest stations are above the law; and, if they can attain the object of their ambition, they have no fear of being called to account for the means by which they acquired it. They often endeavour, therefore, not only by fraud and falsehood — the ordinary and vulgar arts of intrigue and cabal — but sometimes by the perpetration of the most enormous crimes, by murder and assassination, by rebellion and civil war, to supplant and destroy those who oppose or stand in the way of their greatness. They more frequently miscarry than succeed, and commonly gain nothing but the disgraceful punishment which is due to their crimes. But, though they should be so lucky as to attain that wished-for-greatness, they are always most miserably disappointed in the happiness which they expect to enjoy in it. It is not ease or pleasure, but always honour of one kind or another, though frequently an honour very ill understood, that the ambitious man really pursues. But the honour of his exalted station appears both in his own eyes and in those of other people polluted and defiled by the baseness of the means through which he rose to it. Though by the profusion of every liberal expense, though by excessive indulgence in every profligate pleasure, the wretched but usual resource of ruined characters, though by the hurry of public business, or by the prouder and more dazzling tumult of war, he may endeavour to efface both from his own memory and from that of other people the remembrance of what he has done — that remembrance never fails to pursue him. He invokes in vain the dark and dismal powers of forgetfulness and oblivion. He remembers himself what he has done, and that remembrance tells him that other people must likewise remember it. Amidst all the gaudy pomp of the most ostentatious greatness, amidst the venal and vile adulation of the great and of the learned, amidst the more innocent, though more foolish, acclamations of the common people, amidst all the pride of conquest and the triumph of successful war, he is still secretly pursued by the avenging furies of shame and remorse; and, while glory seems to surround him on all sides, he himself, in his own imagination, sees black and foul infamy fast pursuing him and every moment ready to overtake him from behind. Even the great Caesar, though he had the magnanimity to dismiss his guards, could not dismiss his suspicions. The remembrance of Pharsalia still haunted and pursued him. When, at the request of the senate, he had the generosity to pardon Marcellus, he told that assembly that he was not unaware of the designs which were carrying on against his life, but that, as he had lived long enough both for nature and for glory, he was contented to die and therefore despised all conspiracies. He had, perhaps, lived long enough for nature; but the man who felt himself the object of such deadly resentment from those whose favour he wished to gain, and whom he still wished to consider as his friends, had certainly lived too long for real glory, or for all the happiness which he could ever hope to enjoy in the love and esteem of his equals.

Source: from *Adam Smith's Moral and Political Philosophy,* ed. Herbert W. Schneider (Hafner, New York, 1948) pp. 91-107.

9 THE ORIGIN OF THE DISTINCTION OF RANKS

John Millar

Circumstances, which contribute to advance the privileges of the people

In that early period of agriculture when manufacturers are unknown, persons who have no landed estate are usually incapable of procuring subsistence otherwise than by serving some opulent neighbour, by whom they are employed, according to their qualifications, either in military service, or in the several branches of husbandry. Men of great fortune find that the entertaining a multitude of servants, for either of these purposes, is highly conducive both to their dignity and their personal security; and in a rude age, when people are strangers to luxury, and are maintained from the simple productions of the earth, the number of retainers who may be supported upon any particular estate is proportionably great.

In this situation, persons of low rank, have no opportunity of acquiring an affluent fortune, or of raising themselves to superior stations; and remaining for ages in a state of dependence, they naturally contract such dispositions and habits are as suited to their circumstances. They acquire a sacred veneration for the person of their master, and are taught to pay an unbounded submission to his authority. They are proud of that servile obedience by which they seem to exalt his dignity, and consider it as their duty to sacrifice their lives and their possessions in order to promote his interest, or even to gratify his capricious humour.

But when the arts begin to be cultivated in a country, the labouring part of the inhabitants are enabled to procure subsistence in a different manner. They are led to make proficiency in particular trades and professions; and, instead of becoming servants to any body, they often find it more profitable to work at their own charges, and to vend the product of their labour. As in this situation their gain depends upon a variety of customers, they have little to fear from the displeasure of any single person; and, according to the good quality and cheapness of the commodity which they have to dispose of, they may commonly be assured of success in their business.

The farther a nation advances in opulence and refinement, it has occasion to employ a greater number of merchants, of tradesmen and artificers; and as the lower people, in general, become thereby more independent in their circumstances, they begin to exert those sentiments of liberty which are natural to the mind of man, and which necessity alone is able to subdue. In proportion as they have less need of the favour and patronage of the great, they are at less pains to procure it; and their application is more uniformly directed to acquire those talents which are useful in the exercise of their employments. The impressions which they received in their former state of servitude are therefore gradually obliterated, and give place to habits of a different nature. The long attention and perseverance, by which they become expert and skilful in their business, render them ignorant of those decorums and of that politeness which arises from the intercourse of society; and that vanity which was formerly discovered in magnifying the power of a chief, is now equally displayed in sullen indifference, or in contemptuous and insolent behaviour to persons of superior rank and station.

While, from these causes, people of low rank are gradually advancing towards a state of independence, the influence derived from wealth is diminished in the same proportion. From the improvement of arts and manufactures, the ancient simplicity of manners is in a great measure destroyed; and the proprietor of a landed estate, instead of consuming its produce in hiring retainers, is obliged to employ a great part of it in purchasing those comforts and conveniences which have become objects of attention, and which are thought suitable to his condition. Thus while fewer persons are under the necessity of depending upon him, he is daily rendered less capable of maintaining dependents; till at last his domestics and servants are reduced to such as are merely subservient to luxury and pageantry, but are of no use in supporting his authority.

From the usual effects of luxury and refinement, it may at the same time be expected that old families will often be reduced to poverty and beggary. In a refined and luxurious nation those who are born to great affluence, and who have been bred to no business, are excited, with mutual emulation, to surpass one another in the elegance and refinement of their living. According as they have the means of indulging themselves in pleasure, they become more addicted to the pursuit of it, and are sunk in a degree of indolence and dissipation which renders them incapable of any active employment. Thus the expense of the landed gentleman is apt to be continually increasing, without any proportional addition to his income. His estate therefore, being more and more incumbered with debts, is at length alienated, and brought into the possession of the frugal and industrious merchant, who, by success in trade, has been enabled to buy it, and who is desirous of obtaining that rank and consequence which landed property is capable of bestowing. The posterity, however, of this new proprietor, having adopted the manners of the landed gentry, are again led, in a few generations, to squander their estate, with a heedless extravagance equal to the parsimony and activity by which it was acquired.

This fluctuation of property, so observable in all commercial countries, and which no prohibitions are capable of preventing, must necessarily weaken the authority of those who are placed in the higher ranks of life. Persons who have lately attained to riches, have no opportunity of establishing that train of dependence which is maintained by those who have remained for ages at the head of a great estate. The hereditary influence of family is thus, in a great measure, destroyed; and the consideration derived from wealth is often limited to what the possessor can acquire during his own life. Even this too, for the reasons formerly mentioned, is greatly diminished. A man of great fortune having dismissed his retainers, and spending a great part of his income in the purchase of commodities produced by tradesmen and manufacturers, has no ground to expect that many persons will be willing either to fight for him, or to run any great hazard for promoting his interest. Whatever profit he means to obtain from the labour and assistance of others, he must give a full equivalent for it. He must buy those personal services which are no longer to be performed either from attachment or from peculiar connexions. Money, therefore, becomes more and more the only means of procuring honours and dignities; and the sordid pursuits of avarice are made subservient to the nobler purposes of ambition.

It cannot be doubted that these circumstances have a tendency to introduce a democratical government. As persons of inferior rank are placed in a situation which, in point of subsistence, renders them little dependent upon their superiors; as no one order of men continues in the exclusive possession of opulence; and as every man who is industrious may entertain the hope of gaining a fortune; it is to be expected that the prerogatives of the monarch and of the ancient nobility will be gradually undermined, that the privileges of the people will be extended in the same proportion, and that power, the usual attendant of wealth, will be in some measure diffused over all the members of the community.

Result of the opposition between these different principles

So widely different are the effects of opulence and refinement, which, at the same time that they furnish the king with a standing army, the great engine of tyranny and oppression, have also a tendency to inspire the people with notions of liberty and independence. It may thence be expected that a conflict will arise between these two opposite parties, in which a variety of accidents may contribute to cast the balance upon either side.

With respect to the issue of such a contest, it may be remarked that, in a small state, the people have been commonly successful in their efforts to establish a free constitution. When a state consists only of a small territory, and the bulk of the inhabitants live in one city, they have frequently occasion to converse together, and to communicate their sentiments upon every subject of importance. Their attention therefore is roused by every instance of oppression in the government; and as they easily take the alarm, so they are capable of quickly uniting their forces in order to demand redress of their grievances. By repeated experiments they become sensible of their strength, and are enabled by degrees to enlarge their privileges, and to assume a greater share of the public administration.

In large and extensive nations, the struggles between the sovereign and his people are, on the contrary, more likely to terminate in favour of despotism. In a wide country, the encroachments of the government are frequently over-looked; and, even when the indignation of the people has been roused by flagrant injustice, they find it difficult to combine in uniform and vigorous measures for the defence of their rights. It is also difficult, in a great nation, to bring out the militia with that quickness which is requisite in case of a sudden invasion; and it becomes necessary, even before the country has been much civilized, to maintain such a body of mercenaries as is capable of supporting the regal authority.

It is farther to be considered that the revenue of the monarch is commonly a more powerful engine of authority in a great nation than in a small one. The influence of a sovereign seems to depend, not so much upon his absolute wealth, as upon the proportion which it bears to that of the other members of the community. So far as the estate of the king does not exceed that of the richest of his subjects, it is no more than sufficient to supply the ordinary expense of living, in a manner suitable to the splendour and dignity of the crown; and it is only the surplus of that estate which can be directly applied to the purposes of creating dependence. In this view the public revenue of the king will be productive of greater influence according to the extent and populousness of the country in which it is raised. Suppose in a country, like that of ancient Attica, containing about twenty thousand inhabitants, the people were, by assessment or otherwise, to pay at the rate of twenty shillings each person, this would produce only twenty thousand pounds; a revenue that would probably not exalt the chief magistrate above many private citizens. But in a kingdom, containing ten millions of people, the taxes, being paid in the same proportion, would in all probability render the estate of the monarch superior to the united wealth of many hundreds of the most opulent individuals. In these two cases therefore, the disproportion of the armies maintained in each kingdom should be greater than that of their respective revenues; and if in the one, the king was enabled to maintain two hundred and fifty thousand men, he would in the other, be incapable of supporting the expense of five hundred. It is obvious, however, that even five hundred regular and well disciplined troops will not strike the same terror into twenty thousand people, that will be created, by an army of two hundred and fifty thousand, over a nation composed of ten millions.

Most of the ancient republics, with which we are acquainted, appear to have owed their liberty to the narrowness of their territories. From the small number of people, and from the close intercourse among all the individuals in the same community, they imbibed a spirit of freedom even before they had made considerable progress in arts; and they found means to repress or abolish the power of their petty princes, before their effeminacy or industry had introduced the practice of maintaining mercenary troops.

The same observation is applicable to the modern states of Italy, who, after the decay of the western empire, began to flourish in trade, and among whom a republican form of government was early established.

In France, on the other hand, the introduction of a great mercenary army, during the administration of Cardinal Richelieu, which was necessary for the defence of the country, enabled the monarch to establish a despotical power. In the beginning of the reign of Lewis XIII was called the last convention of the states general which has ever been held in that country: and the monarch has, from that period, been accustomed to exercise almost all the different powers of government. Similar effects have arisen from the establishment of standing forces in most of the great kingdoms of Europe.

The fortunate situation of Great Britain, after the accession of James I, gave her little to fear from any foreign invasion, and superseded the necessity of maintaining a standing army, when the service of the feudal militia had gone into disuse. The weakness and bigotry of her monarchs, at that period, prevented them from employing the only expedient capable of securing an absolute authority. Charles I saw the power exercised, about his time, by the other princes of Europe; but he did not discover the means by which it was obtained. He seems to have been so much convinced of his divine indefeasible right as, at first, to think that no force was necessary, and afterwards, that every sort of duplicity was excuseable, in support of it. When at the point of a rupture with his parliament, he had no military force upon which he could depend; and he was therefore obliged to yield to the growing power of the commons.

The boldness and dexterity, joined to the want of public spirit, and the perfidy of Oliver Cromwell, rendered abortive the measures of that party, of which he obtained the direction; but the blood that had been shed, and the repeated efforts that were made by the people in defence of their privileges, cherished and spread the love of liberty, and at last produced a popular government, after the best model, perhaps, which is practicable in an extensive country.

Many writers appear to take pleasure in remarking that, as the love of liberty is natural to man, it is to be found in the greatest perfection among barbarians, and is apt to be impaired according as people make progress in civilization and in the arts of life. That mankind, in the state of mere savages, are in great measure unacquainted with government, and unaccustomed to any sort of constraint, is sufficiently evident. But their independence, in that case, is owing to the wretchedness of their circumstances, which afford nothing that can tempt any one man to become subject to another. The moment they have quitted this primitive situation, and, by endeavouring to supply their natural wants, have been led to accumulate property, they are presented with very different motives of action, and acquire a new set of habits and principles. In those rude ages when the inhabitants of the earth are divided into tribes of shepherds, or of husbandmen, the usual distribution of property renders the bulk of the people dependent upon a few chiefs, to whom fidelity and submission becomes the principal point of honour, and makes a distinguishing part of the national character. The ancient Germans, whose high notions of freedom have been the subject of many a well-turned period, were accustomed, as we learn from Tacitus, to stake their persons upon the issue of a game of hazard, and after an unlucky turn of fortune, to yield themselves up to a voluntary servitude. Wherever men of inferior condition are enabled to live in affluence by their own industry, and, in procuring their livelihood, have little occasion to court the favour of their superiors, there we may expect that ideas of liberty will be universally diffused. This happy arrangement of things, is naturally produced by commerce and manufactures; but it would be as vain to look for it in the uncultivated parts of the world, as to look for the independent spirit of an English waggoner, among persons of low rank in the highlands of Scotland. . . .

The condition of servants in the primitive ages of the world

From the situation of mankind in rude and barbarous countries, we may easily conceive in what manner any one person is, at first, reduced to be the servant of another. Before the manners of men are civilized, and a regular government has been established, persons of small fortune are subject to great inconveniencies from the disorder and violence of the times, and are frequently obliged to solicit the assistance and protection of some powerful neighbour, by whom they are entertained in the station of vassals or military dependents. But those who, from their idleness, have acquired nothing, or who, by accident, have been deprived of their possessions, are necessarily exposed to much more severe calamities. They have no room or encouragement for the exercise of those beneficial trades and professions, the effects of luxury and refinement, by which, in a polished nation, a multitude of people are enabled to live in a comfortable manner. In many cases, therefore, they are under the necessity of serving some opulent person, who, upon account of their labour, is willing to maintain them; and as they are entirely dependent upon him for their subsistence, they are engaged according to his circumstances, and according to the qualifications they possess, in all the mean and servile occupations which may be requisite for the convenience and support of his family.

In early ages, when neighbouring tribes or nations are almost continually engaged in mutual hostilities, it frequently happens that one of the parties, is totally reduced under the power of another. The use that is made of a victory, upon these occasions, is such as might be expected from a fierce and barbarous people, who have too little experience or reflection to discover the utility of carrying on the trade of war with some degree of humanity. The vanquished are often put to death, in order to gratify a spirit of revenge; or, if they are spared, it is only from the consideration that their future labour and service will be of more advantage to the conqueror. As in those times every individual goes out to battle at his own charges, so he claims a proportional share of the profits arising from the expedition; and of consequence obtains the absolute disposal of the captives whom he has procured by his valour, or who, in a division of the booty, are bestowed upon him as the reward of his merit. . . .

By . . . captivity, by the voluntary submission of the indigent, or by the sentence of a judge, many are reduced into a state of unlimited subjection, and become the servants of those who are opulent and prosperous. It may be questioned, in such a case, how far a person is intitled to make use of that power which fortune has put into his hands. It is difficult to ascertain the degree of authority which, from the principles of justice and humanity, we are, in any situation, permitted to assume over our fellow-creatures. But the fact admits of no question, that people have commonly been disposed to use their power in such a manner as appears most conducive to their interest, and most agreeable to their predominant passions. It is natural to suppose that the master would let no bounds to his prerogative over those unhappy persons who, from their circumstances, were under the necessity of yielding an implicit obedience to his commands. He forced them to labour as much, and gave them as little in return for it as possible. When he found them negligent of their employment, he bestowed upon them such correction as he thought proper; and, actuated by the boisterous dispositions of a savage, he was in some cases provoked to chastise them with a degree of severity, by which they might even be deprived of their life. When he had no use for their work, or when a good opportunity was presented, he endeavoured by a sale to dispose of them to the highest advantage. When he chose to increase the number of his servants, he sometimes encouraged and directed their multiplication; and the same authority which he exercised over the parents was extended to their offspring, whom he had been at the trouble of rearing, and who were equally dependent upon him for their subsistence.

To be a servant, therefore, in those primitive times, was almost universally the same thing as to be a slave. The master assumed an unlimited jurisdiction over his servants, and the privilege of selling them at pleasure. He gave them no wages beside their maintenance; and he allowed them to have no property, but claimed to his own use whatever, by their labour or by any other means, they happened to acquire.

Thus the practice of domestic slavery appears to have been early established among the nations of antiquity; among the Egyptians, the Phoenicians, the Jews, the Babylonians, the Persians, the Greeks, and the Romans.

The same practice obtains at present among all those tribes of barbarians, in different parts of the world, with which we have any correspondence.

There are indeed but few slaves among the greater part of the savages of America; because, from the situation of that people, they have no opportunity of accumulating wealth for maintaining any number of servants. As, in ordinary cases, they find it burdensome to give subsistence to an enemy whom they have subdued, they are accustomed to indulge their natural ferocity by putting him to death, even in cold blood. If ever they behave with humanity to their captives, it is only when being greatly reduced by the calamities of war, or by uncommon accidents, they are under the immediate necessity of recruiting their strength; and as this rarely happens, the persons whose lives have been thus preserved, are not distinguished from the children of the family into which they are brought, but are formally adopted into the place of the deceased relations, whose loss they are intended to supply.

The Tartars, on the other hand, who have great possessions in herds and flocks, find no difficulty in supporting a number of domestics. For this reason they commonly preserve their captives, with a view of reaping the benefit that may arise from their labour; and the servitude established among that people disposes them to treat their enemies with a degree of moderation, which otherwise could hardly be expected from their fierce and barbarous dispositions.

The same observation may be extended to the negroes upon the coast of Guinea, who, from their intercourse with the nations of Europe, derive yet greater advantages from sparing the lives of their enemies. At the same time it cannot be doubted, that, as the encounters of those barbarians have upon this account become less bloody, their wars have been rendered more frequent. From the great demand for slaves to supply the European market, they have the same motives to seize the person of their neighbours, which may excite the inhabitants of other countries to rob one another of their property.

The usual effects of opulence and civilized manners, with regard to the treatment of servants

These institutions and customs are such as might be expected from the limited experience, as well as from the rude manners of an early age. By reducing his servants into a state of slavery, the master appears, at first sight, to reap the highest advantage from their future labour and service. But when a people become civilized, and when they have made considerable progress in commerce and manufactures, one would imagine they should entertain more liberal views, and be influenced by more extensive considerations of utility.

A slave, who receives no wages in return for his labour, can never be supposed to exert much vigour or activity in the exercise of any employment. He obtains a livelihood at any rate; and by his utmost assiduity he is able to procure no more. As he works merely in consequence of the terror in which he is held, it may be imagined that he will be idle as often as he can with impunity. This circumstance may easily be overlooked in a country where the inhabitants are strangers to improvement. But when the arts begin to flourish, when the wonderful effects of industry and skill in cheapening commodities, and in bringing them to perfection, become more and more conspicuous, it must be evident that little profit can be drawn from the labour of a slave, who has neither been encouraged to acquire that dexterity, nor those habits of application, which are essentially requisite in the finer and more difficult branches of manufacture.

This may be illustrated from the price of labour in our West-India islands, where it will not be doubted that the inhabitants are at great pains to prevent the idleness of their slaves. In Jamaica, the yearly labour of a field-negro, when he is upheld to the master, is rated at no more than nine pounds, currency of that island. When a negro has been instructed in the trade of a carpenter, the value of his yearly labour will amount at the utmost to thirty-six pounds; whereas a free man is capable of earning seventy pounds yearly in the very same employment.

It is further to be observed, that, in a polished nation, the acquisition of slaves is commonly much more expensive than among a simple and barbarous people.

After a regular government has been established, the inhabitants of a country are restrained from plundering one another; and, under the authority of the magistrate, individuals of the lowest rank are sufficiently secured from oppression and injustice. In proportion to the improvement of commerce and manufactures, the demand for labour is increased, and greater encouragement is given to industry. The poor have more resources for procuring a livelihood, by such employments as are productive of little subjection or dependence. By degrees, therefore, people of inferior condition are freed from the necessity of becoming slaves in order to obtain subsistence; and the ancient agreement by which a free person resigned his liberty, and was reduced under the power of a master, being rendered more and more unusual, is at length regarded as inconsistent with the natural rights of a citizen.

[1] Thus among the Romans, during the commonwealth, and even under the emperors, no free citizen was allowed, by contract, to become the slave of another. [2] It was consistent with the refined laws of that people, which rescinded those unequal contracts where one party had gained an undue advantage, or even obtained an unreasonable profit at the expense of the other, to declare that bargain by which a man surrendered all his rights to a master, and consequently received nothing in return, should have no support or encouragement from the civil magistrate.

As men begin to experience the happy effects of cultivating the arts of peace, and are less frequently employed in acts of hostility, they have less occasion to acquire any number of slaves by captivity. The influence of civilization upon the temper and dispositions of a people has at the same time a tendency to produce a total revolution in the manner of conducting their military operations. That ancient institution, by which every one who is able to bear arms is required to appear in the field at his own charges, becomes too heavy a burden upon those who are enervated with pleasure, or engaged in lucrative professions; and the custom of employing mercenary troops in defence of the country is therefore gradually established. As an army of this kind is maintained by the government; as the soldiers receive constant pay, which is understood to be a full equivalent for their service; they appear to have no title to the extraordinary emoluments arising from the spoil of the enemy; and therefore the captives, though reduced into servitude, are no longer held as belonging to those particular persons by whom they have been subdued, but to the public, at whose expense and hazard the

---

[1] (Part lifted out of footnote; part new)

[2] See Heineccius, Ant. Rom. lib. I, tit. 5, 6. This regulation, however, admitted of an exception, where a man fraudulently suffered himself to be sold in order to share in the price; in which case he became the slave of the person whom he had defrauded. L. 3. Dig. quib. ad. libert. proclam. non licet.

war is supported.

We may take notice of a similar change in the acquisition of slaves by the sentence of a judge. In rude times, the chief aim of punishment was to gratify the resentment of the private party; and if a person accused of a crime had been found guilty, he was, for that reason, frequently delivered up as a slave to the plaintiff. But upon greater improvement of manners, the interpositions of the magistrate came to be influenced more by considerations of general utility; and as the crimes of individuals were principally considered in the light of offences against the society, it was agreeable to this idea that a criminal should become the slave of the public, and should either be employed in public works, or disposed of in the manner most advantageous to the revenue of the community.

The inhabitants of a civilized country, being thus in a great measure deprived of the primitive modes of acquisition, are obliged to acquire the bulk of their slaves, either by a purchase from their poorer and more barbarous neighbours, or by propagating and rearing from the original stock which they possess. In such a situation, therefore, when we compute the expense attending the labour of a slave, not only the charge of his maintenance, but also the money laid out in the first acquisition, together with all the hazard to which his life is exposed, must necessarily be taken into the account.

When these circumstances are duly considered, it will be found that the work of a slave, who receives nothing but a bare subsistence, is really dearer than that of a free man, to whom constant wages are given in proportion to his industry.

Unhappily, men have seldom been in a condition to examine this point with proper attention, and with sufficient impartiality. The practice of slavery being introduced in an early age, is afterwards regarded with that blind prepossession which is commonly acquired in favour of ancient usages: its inconveniences are overlooked, and every innovation, with respect to it, is considered as a dangerous measure. The possession of power is too agreeable to be easily relinquished. Few people will venture upon a new experiment; and, amidst the general prejudices of a country, fewer still are capable of making it with fairness. We find, accordingly, that this institution, however inconsistent with the rights of humanity, however pernicious and contrary to the true interest of the master, has generally remained in those countries where it was once established, and has been handed down from one generation to another, during all the successive improvements of society, in knowledge, arts, and manufactures.

The advancement of a nation, in these particulars, is even frequently attended with greater severity in the treatment of the slaves. The simplicity of early ages admits of little distinction between the master and his servants, in their employments or manner of living; and though, from the impetuosity and violence of his temper, they may, on some occasions, be subjected to hardships, he enjoys no great superiority over them, in their dress, their lodging, or ordinary entertainment. By the introduction of wealth and luxury, this equality is gradually destroyed. The various refinements which tend to multiply the comforts and conveniencies of life; whatever contributes to ease, to pleasure, to ostentation, or to amusement, is in a great measure appropriate to the rich and the free, while those who remain in a state of servitude are retained in their primitive indigence. The slaves are no longer accustomed to sit at the same table with their master. They must look upon him as a being of superior order, whom they are seldom permitted to approach, and with whom they have hardly any thing in common; who beholds with indifference the toil and drudgery to which they are subjected, and from whom they can with difficulty procure a scanty subsistence. ...

Causes of the freedom acquired by the labouring people in the modern nations of Europe

By what happy concurrence of events has the practice of slavery been so generally abolished in Europe? By what powerful motives were our forefathers induced to deviate from the maxims of other nations, and to abandon a custom so generally retained in other parts of the world?

The northern barbarians, who laid the foundation of the present European states, are said to have possessed a number of slaves, obtained either by captivity or by voluntary submission, and over whom the master enjoyed an unlimited authority.

When these nations invaded the Roman empire, and settled in the different provinces, they were enabled by their repeated victories to procure an immense number of captives, whom they reduced into servitude, and by whose assistance they occupied landed estates of proportionable extent. From the simple manner of living to which those barbarians had been accustomed, their domestic business was usually performed by the members of each family; and their servants, for the most part, were employed in cultivating their lands. ...

The situation, however, of these bond-men, and the nature of the employment in which they were usually engaged, had a tendency to procure them a variety of privileges from their master, by which, in a course of ages, their condition was rendered more comfortable, and they were advanced to higher degrees of consideration and rank.

As the peasants belonging to a single person could not be conveniently maintained in his house, so in order to cultivate his lands to advantage, it was necessary that they should be sent to a distance, and have a fixed residence in different parts of his estate. Separate habitations were therefore assigned them; and particular farms were committed to the care of individuals, who from their residing in the neighbourhood of one another, and forming small villages or hamlets, received the appellation of 'villains'.

It may easily be imagined that, in those circumstances, the proprietor of a large estate could not oversee the behaviour of his servants, living in separate families, and scattered over the wide extent of his demesnes; and it was in vain to think of compelling them to labour by endeavouring to chastise them upon account of their idleness. A very little experience would show that no efforts of that kind could be effectual; and that the only means of exciting the industry of the peasants would be to offer them a reward for the work which they performed. Thus, beside the ordinary maintenance allotted to the slaves, they frequently obtained a small gratuity, which, by custom, was gradually converted into a regular hire; and, being allowed the enjoyment and disposal of that subject, they were at length understood to be capable of having separate property.

After the master came to reside at a distance from the bulk of his servants, and had embraced the salutary policy of bribing them, instead of using compulsion, in order to render them active in their employment, he was less apt to be provoked by their negligence; and as he had seldom occasion to treat them with severity, the ancient dominion which he exercised over their lives was at length entirely lost by disuse.

When a slave had been for a long time engaged in a particular farm, and had become acquainted with that particular culture which it required, he was so much the better qualified to continue in the management of it for the future; and it was contrary to the interest of the master that he should be removed to another place, or employed in labour of a different kind. By degrees, therefore, the peasants were regarded as belonging to the stock upon the ground, and came to be uniformly disposed of as a part of the estate which they had been accustomed to cultivate. . . .

The effect of the foregoing circumstances is even observable in the history of the Greeks and Romans, among whom the peasants were raised to a better condition than the rest of their slaves. They were indeed bound to serve the proprietor during life, and might have been sold along with the ground upon which they were employed; but their persons were not subject to the absolute jurisdiction of their master; they had the privilege of marrying without his consent; they received wages in return for their labour, and were understood to have a full right of property in whatever goods their industry had enabled them to accumulate.

It should seem, however, that the limited territory possessed by these ancient nations prevented the farther extension of the privileges bestowed upon their peasants: seven acres were originally the utmost extent of landed property which a Roman citizen was permitted to enjoy; a portion which he was able to cultivate with his own hands, or with no other assistance but that of his own family; and there is reason to believe that, for several centuries, no individual acquired such an estate as gave occasion to his retaining many servants for the management of it, or could render the inspection and government of those whom he employed a matter of great trouble or difficulty.

But after the wide and populous countries under the Roman dominion were subdued and laid waste by the small tribes of the Germans, very extensive landed estates, together with an adequate number of slaves, were immediately acquired by particular persons. As the people retained their primitive simplicity of manners, and were in a great measure strangers to commerce, these large possessions remained for ages without being dismembered. And thus, during all the successive improvements of agriculture, the proprietor of an estate, embarrassed with the multitude of his villains, was obliged to repose a confidence in them, and came by degrees to discover more clearly the utility of exciting them to industry by the prospect of their own private advantage.

The same motives, by which the master was induced to reward his slaves for their labour, determined him afterwards to increase his bounty in proportion to the work which they performed. Having no opportunity of looking narrowly into their management, he was commonly led to estimate their diligence according to their success; and therefore, when they brought him a good crop, he made an addition to their wages, at the same time that he allowed them to expect a suitable compensation for their future labour and economy. This at length gave rise to an express stipulation, that their profits should depend upon the fertility of their different farms, and that, in all cases, they should be permitted to retain a certain share of the produce, in consideration of their labour.

An expedient so obvious and well calculated for promoting the industry of the peasants, could hardly fail to be generally embraced in all the countries of Europe, as soon as the inhabitants became attentive to the improvement of their estates. The remains of this practice are still to be found in Scotland, where, in some cases, the landlord is accustomed to stock the farm, and the tenant pays him a rent in kind, consisting of a certain proportion of the fruits.

By this alteration, the villains entered into a sort of co-partnership with their master; and having always a prospect of gain, according to the vigour or talents which they exerted, they were enabled to earn a more comfortable subsistence, and were even gradually raised to affluence. The acquisition of wealth paved the way to a further extension of their privileges. Those who had obtained something considerable found themselves in a condition to stock their own farms, and to offer a fixed rent to the master, upon condition of their being allowed to retain the surplus for their own emolument. An agreement of this kind, so advantageous to both parties, was concluded without any difficulty. As the tenant secured to himself the whole profit arising from his industry, the landlord was freed from the hazard of accidental losses, and obtained not only a certain, but frequently an additional revenue from his lands.

Thus, by degrees, the ancient villanage came to be entirely abolished. The peasants, who cultivated their farms at their own charges, and at their own hazard, were of course emancipated from the authority of their master, and could no longer be regarded as in the condition of servants. Their personal subjection was at an end. It was of no consequence to the landlord how they conducted themselves; and, provided they punctually paid his rent, nothing farther could be required of them. There was no reason to insist that they should remain in the farm longer than they pleased; for the profits it afforded made them, commonly, not more willing to leave it than the proprietor was to put them away. When agriculture became so beneficial a trade, when the state of those who followed that profession had been rendered so comfortable, no person had any difficulty to procure a sufficient number of tenants to labour his estate. It was, on the contrary, sometimes difficult for the farmer to obtain land sufficient for the exercise of his employment; and, after he had been at pains to improve the soil, he was in danger of being dispossessed by the proprietor, before he was indemnified for the trouble and expense which he had sustained. This made it necessary to stipulate that he should be allowed to remain for a certain time in the possession, and gave rise to leases, for a term of years, and even sometimes for life, or for a longer period, according to the circumstances or inclination of the parties.

The modern nations of Europe continued for a long time to be almost entirely unacquainted with manufactures; and, as they had no other slaves but those which were employed in agriculture, the privileges acquired by the villains had therefore a tendency to produce a total extinction of servitude. By degrees, however, as the people began to improve their circumstances, and to multiply the comforts and conveniencies of life, their attention was more and more diverted to other employments. At the same time that the villains were engaged in cultivating the ground, they were also bound to perform any other services which the master thought proper to require, and were often called to assist him in the practice of those few mechanical arts which were then understood. Particular persons acquiring a singular dexterity in these occupations, were distinguished upon that account, and came to be more frequently employed than their neighbours. In proportion to the liberty which they enjoyed as peasants, they were enabled with more advantage to prosecute this collateral business; and while they received a reward for the crop which they produced upon their farms, they were not restrained from working, for hire, in that peculiar trade or profession which they were qualified to exercise. As the progress of luxury and refinement multiplied these occupations, and rendered the profits which they afforded superior in many cases to those which were derived from agriculture, individuals were gradually led to quit the latter employment, and to attach themselves entirely to the former. In that state of the country, the children of farmers were frequently bred to manufactures; and a number of tradesmen and artificers, having arisen in different villages, were advanced to consideration and esteem, in proportion as their assistance became more essentially necessary, in supplying the wants of mankind. According to the wealth which this new order of men had accumulated, they purchased immunities from their master; and, by permitting him to levy tolls and duties upon their commerce, they were enabled to secure his patronage and protection. Thus the privileges acquired by the peasants appear to have given rise to domestic freedom, which was communicated to the trading part of the inhabitants; while the employment of the latter became, on the other hand, the source of great opulence, and contributed, as has been formerly observed, to raise the people of inferior rank to political independence. .

By the progress of improvements in the arts and crafts a greater proportion of the inhabitants, instead of living as retainers or servants of the rich, became engaged in various mechanical employments, or in different branches of traffic, from which they could earn a livelihood without the necessity of courting the favour of their superiors. An artificer, whose labour is enhanced by the general demand for it, or a tradesman who sells his goods in a common market, considers himself as his own master. He says that he is obliged to his employers, or his customers; and he treats them with civility; but he does not feel himself greatly dependent upon them. His subsistence, and his profits, are derived not from one, but from a number of persons; he knows, besides, that their employment or their custom proceeds not commonly from personal favour, but from a regard to their own interest; and consequently that, while he serves them equally well, he has no reason to apprehend the decline of his business. Rising more and more to this independent situation, artificers and tradesmen were led by degrees to shake off their ancient slavish habits, to gratify their own inclinations or humours, and to indulge that love of liberty, so congenial to the mind of man, which nothing but imperious necessity is able to subdue.

The independence and the influence of this order of people was farther promoted by the circumstance of their being collected in towns, whence they derived an extreme facility in communicating their sentiments and opinions. In a populous city, not only the discoveries and knowledge, but the feelings and passions of each individual are quickly and readily propagated over the whole. If an injury is committed, if an act of oppression is complained of, it immediately spreads an alarm, becomes the subject of clamour and censure, and excites the general indignation and resentment. Everyone roused by the example of those around him, loses the sense of his own danger in the ardour and impetuosity of his companions. Some bold and enterprising leader acquires an ascendancy over their common movements; and while their first impressions are yet warm, finds no difficulty in uniting them to defend their privileges, or to demand redress for their wrongs.

While the tradesmen, manufacturers, and merchants of England, were thus rapidly increasing in number, and advancing to such comfortable situations, many individuals in those classes were, by successful industry in the more lucrative branches of trade, and by a rigid and persevering economy, the natural effect of their habits, enabled to acquire splendid fortunes, and to reflect a degree of lustre upon the profession to which they belonged. In this, as in all other cases, property became the source of consideration and respect; and, in proportion as the trading part of the nation became opulent they obtained more weight in the community.

The progressive advancement to freedom and independence of the manufacturing and mercantile people was followed, in the natural course of things, by that of the peasantry or farmers, the other great class of the commonalty. From the multiplication of the trading towns, and their increasing population and riches, the consumption of all the necessaries of life was promoted, and the market for every species of provisions proportionably extended. The price of every article produced by the land was therefore enhanced by a greater competition of purchasers; and the labour of those persons employed in agriculture was called forth and rewarded by an augmentation of profits; not to mention, that the activity and enterprising genius of merchants, arising from their large capitals, their extensive dealings, and their mutual intercourse, were naturally communicated to the neighbouring farmers; who, from the limited nature of their undertakings, and from their dispersed and solitary residence, trusting to the slow experience and detached observations of each individual, were likely, independent of this additional excitement, to proceed with great caution and timidity, and therefore to advance very slowly in the knowledge of their profession. In proportion to the general improvement of agriculture, it was expected that farmers should undertake more expensive operations in manuring and meliorating their grounds; and to encourage these undertakings, the master found it necessary to give them a reasonable prospect of indemnity, by securing them for an adequate length of time in the possession of their farms. By the extension of leases of land, which became more and more universal, the farmers of England not only were emancipated from their primitive dependence, but acquired a degree of rank and importance unknown in most other countries.

The same causes which exalted the common people, diminished the influence of the nobility, or of such as were born to great fortunes. The improvement of arts, the diffusion of all those accommodations which are the natural consequence of that improvement, were accompanied with a change of manners; the ancient plainness and simplicity giving place by degrees to a relish for pleasure and to a taste of luxury and refinement, which were productive of greater expense in all the articles of living. Men of high rank, who found themselves, without any exertion of their own possessed of great wealth, were not prompted by their situation to acquire habits either of industry or of economy. To live upon their estates, to pass their time in idleness, or to follow their amusement, was regarded as their birth-right. Gaining nothing, therefore, by their industry, and exposed by the growing luxury of the times to the daily temptation of increasing their expenses, they were, of course, involved in difficulties, were obliged to devise expedients for raising money, and reduced to the necessity of purchasing an additional rent, by granting long leases, or even more permanent rights to their tenants. The ancient retainers, whom every feudal baron had been accustomed to maintain upon his estate for the purpose of defending him against all his enemies, were unavoidably dismissed; and the military services, which had been formerly exacted from the vassals, were converted into stated pecuniary payments. These conversions, indeed, were at the same time recommended from the change of manners and the alterations in the state of the country; as, by the suppression of private feuds among the great lords, and the general establishment of peace and tranquillity, the maintainence of such retainers, on account of personal defence, had become superfluous.

The nobility, or great barons, were thus deprived of that armed force, and of that multitude of adherents and dependents by which they had formerly supported their authority and dignity. Many individuals among them, from the progress of dissipation and extravagance, were at length obliged, upon the failure of other resources, to contract debts, to mortgage, and to squander away their estates. The frugal and industrious merchant, who had acquired a fortune by trade, was enabled, in such a case, to purchase what the idle and extravagant proprietor found it necessary to sell. Property in land, originally the great source of influence, was in this manner transferred from the higher to the lower classes; the character of the trader and that of the landed gentleman were in some measure confounded; and the consideration and rank of the latter were, by a change of circumstances, communicated to the former.

These gradual changes in the state of the country could not fail to affect the condition of the monarch, as well as the authority of parliament, and, in particular, the relative weight of the two houses.

The improvement of arts, and the progress of luxury and refinement, which increased the rate of living to every nobleman, or private gentleman, had necessarily the same effect upon that of the sovereign. The additional accommodations and pleasures, the various modes of elegance or ostentation, which the fashion of the times was daily introducing, occasioned a proportional addition to the expense requisite for supporting the king's household, and maintaining the dignity of the crown. The different officers and servants employed in all the branches of public business, finding their subsistence more expensive than formerly, required of course an augmentation of salaries or emoluments. From the advancement of society in civilization, from the greater accumulation of property in the hands of individuals, and from a correspondent extension of the connections and pursuits of mankind, a more complicated set of regulations became necessary for maintaining good order and tranquillity; and the number of different officers and servants in the various departments of administration was unavoidably augmented. Upon all these accounts, the king, who found his ancient revenue more and more inadequate to his expenses, was laid under greater difficulties in supporting the machine of government, and obliged more frequently to solicit the aid of parliament for obtaining additional supplies.

In England, as well as in other European countries which had made considerable progress in arts and manufactures, we may discover the operation of two principles which had an opposite political tendency; the independence and opulence acquired by the lower classes of the people, which tended to produce a popular government; and the introduction of mercenary armies for the purpose of national defence, which contributed to extend and support the power of the crown. This gave rise, unavoidably, to a contest between the king and the people; while the former was endeavouring to extend his prerogative, and the latter to maintain or augment their privileges. ...

From the limited powers both of the mind and the body, the exertions of an individual are likely to be more vigorous and successful when confined to a particular channel, than when diffused over a boundless expanse. The athlete who limited his application to one of the gymnastic exercises, was commonly enabled to practice it with more dexterity than he who studied to become proficient in them all.

But though the separation of different trades and professions, together with the consequent division of labour and application in the exercise of them, has a tendency to improve every art or science, it has frequently an opposite effect upon the personal qualities of those individuals who are engaged in such employments. In the sciences, indeed, and even in the liberal arts, the application of those who follow particular professions can seldom be so much limited as to prove destructive to general knowledge. But the mechanical arts admit such minute divisions of labour, that the workmen belonging to a manufacture are each of them employed, for the most part, in a single manual operation, and have no concern in the result of their several productions. It is hardly possible that these mechanics should acquire extensive information or intelligence. In proportion as the operation which they perform is narrow, it will supply them with few ideas; and according as the necessity of obtaining a livelihood obliges them to double their industry, they have the less opportunity or leisure to procure the means of observation, or to find topics of reflection from other quarters. As their employment requires constant attention to an object which can afford no variety of occupation to their minds, they are apt to acquire an habitual vacancy of thought, unenlivened by any prospects, but such as are derived from the future wages of their labour, or from the grateful returns of bodily repose and sleep. They become, like machines, actuated by a regular weight, and performing certain movements with great celerity and exactness, but of small compass, and unfitted for any other use. In the intervals of their work, they can draw but little improvement from the society of companions, bred to similar employments, with whom, if they have much intercourse, they are most likely to seek amusement in drinking and dissipation.

Even in the same country there is a sensible difference between different professions; and, according as every separate employment gives rise to a greater subdivision of workmen and artificers, it has a greater tendency to withdraw from them the means of intellectual improvement. The business of agriculture, for example, is less capable of a minute subdivision of labour than the greater part of mechanical employments. The same workman has often occasion to plough, to sow, and to reap; to cultivate the ground for different purposes, and to prepare its various productions for the market. He is obliged alternately to handle very opposite tools and instruments; to repair, and even sometimes, to make them for his own use; and always to accommodate the different parts of his labour to the change of the seasons and to the variations of the weather. He is employed, in the management and rearing of cattle, becomes frequently a grazier and a corn-merchant, and is unavoidably initiated in the mysteries of the horse-jockey. What an extent of knowledge, therefore, must he possess! What a diversity of talents must he exercise, in comparison with the mechanic, who employs his whole labour in sharpening the point, or in putting on the head of a pin? How different the education of those two persons! The pin-maker, who commonly lives in a town, will have more of the fashionable improvements of society than the peasant; he will undoubtedly be better dressed; he will, in all probability, have more book-learning, as well as less coarseness in the tone of his voice, and less uncouthness in his appearance and deportment. But in a bargain, he would, assuredly, be no match for his rival. He would be greatly inferior in real intelligence and acuteness; much less qualified to converse with his superiors, to take advantage of their foibles, to give a plausible account of his measures, or to adapt his behaviour to any peculiar and unexpected emergency.

The circumstance now mentioned affords a view not very pleasant in the history of human society. It were to be wished that wealth and knowledge should go hand in hand, and that the acquisition of the former should lead to the possession of the latter. Considering the state of nations at large, it will, perhaps, be found that opulence and intellectual improvements are pretty well balanced, and that the same progress in commerce and manufactures which occasions an increase of the one, creates a proportional accession of the other. But, among individuals, this distribution of things is far from being so uniformly established; and, in the lower orders of the people, it appears to be completely reversed. The class of mechanics and labourers, by far the most numerous in a commercial nation, are apt, according as they attain more affluent and independent circumstances, to be more withdrawn and debarred from extensive information; and are likely, in proportion as the rest of the community advance in knowledge and literature to be involved in a thicker cloud of ignorance and prejudice. Is there not reason to apprehend, that the common people, instead of sharing the advantages of national prosperity, are thus in danger of losing their importance, of becoming the dupes of their superiors, and of being degraded from the rank which they held in the scale of society?

The doctrine maintained by some politicians, that the ignorance of the labouring people is of advantage, by securing their patience and submission under the yoke which their unequal fortune has imposed upon them, is no less absurd, than it is revolting to all the feelings of humanity. The security derived from so mean a source is temporary and fallacious. It is liable to be undermined by the intrigues of any plausible projector, or suddenly overthrown by the casual breath of popular opinion.

As the circumstances of commercial society are unfavourable to the mental improvements of the populace, it ought to be the great aim of the public to counteract, in this respect, the natural tendency of mechanical employments, and by the institution of schools and seminaries of education, to communicate, as far as possible, to the most useful, but humble class of citizens, that knowledge which their way of life has, in some degree, prevented them from acquiring. It is needless to observe how imperfect such institutions have hitherto been. The principal schools and colleges of Europe have been intended for the benefit merely of the higher orders; and even for this purpose, the greater part of them are not very judiciously modelled. But men of rank and fortune, and in general those who are exempted from bodily labour, have little occasion, in this respect, for the aid of the public, and perhaps would be better supplied, if left, in a great measure, to their own exertion. The execution, however, of a liberal plan for the instruction of the lower orders, would be a valuable addition to those efforts for the maintenance of the poor, for the relief of the diseased and infirm, and for the correction of the malefactor, which have proceeded from the humanity and public spirit of the present age. The parish schools in Scotland, are the only extensive provisions of that nature hitherto known in the island; and though it must be confessed that they are but ill calculated for the purposes of general education, the advantages resulting from them, even in their present state, have been distinctly felt, and very universally acknowledged.

Source: from William C. Lehmann, *John Millar of Glasgow* (Cambridge University Press, London,1960) pp. 289-310, 375-82.

10 PARASITIC AND PRODUCTIVE CLASSES

Henri de Saint-Simon

Suppose that France suddenly lost fifty of her best physicists, chemists, physiologists, mathematicians, poets, painters, sculptors, musicians, writers; fifty of her best mechanical engineers, civil and military engineers, artillery experts, architects, doctors, surgeons, apothecaries, seamen, clockmakers; fifty of her best bankers, two hundred of her best business men, two hundred of her best farmers, fifty of her best ironmasters, arms manufacturers, tanners, dyers, miners, clothmakers, cotton manufacturers, silk-makers, linen-makers, manufacturers of hardware, of pottery and china, of crystal and glass, ship chandlers, carriers, printers, engravers, goldsmiths, and other metal-workers; her fifty best masons, carpenters, joiners, farriers, locksmiths, cutlers, smelters, and a hundred other persons of various unspecified occupations, eminent in the sciences, fine arts, and professions; making in all the three thousand leading scientists, artists, and artisans of France.*

These men are the Frenchmen who are the most essential producers, those who make the most important products, those who direct the enterprises most useful to the nation, those who contribute to its achievements in the sciences, fine arts and professions. They are in the most real sense the flower of French society; they are, above all Frenchmen, the most useful to their country, contribute most to its glory, increasing its civilization and prosperity. The nation would become a lifeless corpse as soon as it lost them. It would immediately fall into a position of inferiority compared with the nations which it now rivals, and would continue to be inferior until this loss had been replaced, until it had grown another head. It would require at least a generation for France to repair this misfortune; for men who are distinguished in work of positive ability are exceptions, and nature is not prodigal of exceptions, particularly in this species.

Let us pass on to another assumption. Suppose that France preserves all the men of genius that she possesses in the sciences, fine arts and professions, but has the misfortune to lose in the same day Monsieur the King's brother, Monseigneur le duc d'Angoulême, Monseigneur le

---

*Artisan usually means an ordinary workman. To avoid circumlocution, I mean by this expression all those who are concerned with material production, viz., farmers, manufacturers, merchants, bankers, and all the clerk and workmen employed by them.

duc de Berry, Monseigneur le duc d'Orléans, Monseigneur le duc de Bourbon, Madame la duchesse d'Angoulême, Madame la duchesse de Berry, Madame la duchesse d'Orléans, Madame la duchesse de Bourbon, and Mademoiselle de Condé. Suppose that France loses at the same time all the great officers of the royal household, all the ministers (with or without portfolio), all the councillors of state, all the chief magistrates, marshals, cardinals, archbishops, bishops, vicars-general, and canons, all the prefects and sub-prefects, all the civil servants, and judges, and, in addition, ten thousand of the richest proprietors who live in the style of nobles.

This mischance would certainly distress the French, because they are kind-hearted, and could not see with indifference the sudden disappearance of a large number of their compatriots. But this loss of thirty-thousand individuals, considered to be the most important in the State, would only grieve them for purely sentimental reasons and would result in no political evil for the State.

In the first place, it would be very easy to fill the vacancies which would be made available. There are plenty of Frenchmen who could fill the function of the King's brother as well as can Monsieur; plenty who could take the place of a Prince as appropriately as Monseigneur le duc d'Angoulême, or Monseigneur le duc d'Orléans, or Monseigneur le duc de Bourbon. There are plenty of Frenchwomen who would be as good princesses as Madame la duchesse d'Angoulême, or Madame la duchesse de Berry, or Mesdames d'Orléans, de Bourbon, and de Condé.

The ante-chambers of the palace are full of courtiers ready to take the place of the great household officials. The army has plenty of soldiers who would be as good leaders as our present Marshals. How many clerks there are who are as good as our ministers? How many administrators who are capable of managing the affairs of the departments better than the existing prefects and sub-prefects? How many barristers who are as good lawyers as our judges? How many vicars as expert as our cardinals, archbishops, bishops, vicars-general, and canons? As for the ten thousand aristocratic landowners, their heirs could need no apprenticeship to do the honours of their drawing-rooms as well as they.

The prosperity of France can only exist through the effects of the progress of the sciences, fine arts and professions. The Princes, the great household officials, the Bishops, Marshals of France, prefects and idle landowners contribute nothing directly to the progress of the sciences, fine arts and professions. Far from contributing they only hinder, since they strive to prolong the supremacy existing to this day of conjectural ideas over positive science. They inevitably harm the prosperity of the nation by depriving, as they do, the scientists, artists, and artisans of the high esteem to which they are properly entitled. They are harmful because they expend their wealth in a way which is of no direct use to the sciences, fine arts, and professions: they are harmful because they are a charge on the national taxation, to the amount of three or four hundred millions under the heading of appointments, pensions, gifts, compensations, for the upkeep of their activities which are useless to the nation.

These suppositions underline the most important fact of present politics: they provide a point of view from which we can see this fact in a flash in all its extent; they show clearly, though indirectly, that our social organization is seriously defective: that men still allow themselves to be governed by violence and ruse, and that the human race (politically speaking) is still sunk in immorality.

The scientists, artists, and artisans, the only men whose work is of positive utility to society, and cost it practically nothing, are kept down by the princes and other rulers who are simply more or less incapable bureaucrats. Those who control honours and other national awards owe, in general, the supremacy they enjoy, to the accident of birth, to flattery, intrigue and other dubious methods.

Those who control public affairs share between them every year one half of the taxes, and they do not even use a third of what they do not pocket personally in a way which benefits the citizen.

These suppositions show that society is a world which is upside down.

The nation holds as a fundamental principle that the poor should be generous to the rich, and that therefore the poorer classes should daily deprive themselves of necessities in order to increase the superfluous luxury of the rich.

The most guilty men, the robbers on the grand scale, who oppress the mass of the citizens, and extract from them three or four hundred millions a year, are given the responsibility of punishing minor offences against society.

Ignorance, superstition, idleness and costly dissipation are the privilege of the leaders of society, and men of ability, hard-working and thrifty, are employed only as inferiors and instruments.

To sum up, in every sphere men of greater ability are subject to the control of men who are incapable. From the point of view of morality, the most immoral men have the responsibility of leading the citizens towards virtue; from the point of view of distributive justice, the most guilty men are appointed to punish minor delinquents.

The mechanism of social organization was inevitably very complicated so long as the majority of individuals remained in a state of ignorance and improvidence which rendered them incapable of administering their own affairs. In this state of incomplete intellectual development they were swayed by brutal passions which urged them to revolt and every kind of anarchy.

In such a situation, which was the necessary prelude to a better social order, it was necessary for the minority to be organized on military lines, to obtain a monopoly of legislation, and so to keep all power to itself, in order to hold the majority in tutelage and subject the nation to strong discipline. Thus the main energies of the community have till now been directed to maintaining itself as a community, and any efforts directed to improving the moral and physical welfare of the nation have necessarily been regarded as secondary.

To-day this state of affairs can and should be completely altered. The main effort should be directed to the improvement of our moral and physical welfare; only a small amount of force is now required to maintain public order, since the majority have become used to work (which eliminates disorder) and now consists of men who have recently proved that they are capable of administering property, whether in land or money.

As the minority no longer has need of force to keep the proletarian class in subordination, the course which it should adopt is as follows:

(1) A policy by which the proletariat will have the strongest interest in maintaining public order.

(2) A policy which aims at making the inheritance of landed property as easy as possible.

(3) A policy which aims at giving the highest political importance to the workers.

Such a policy is quite simple and obvious, if one takes the trouble to judge the situation by one's own intelligence, and to shake off the yoke enforced on our minds by the political principles of our ancestors — principles which were sound and useful in their own day, but are no longer applicable to present circumstances. The mass of the population is now composed of men (apart from exceptions which occur more or less equally in every class) who are capable of administering property whether in land or in money, and therefore we can and must work directly for the improvement of the moral and physical welfare of the community.

Men are not as bad as they think they are: they are more severe on themselves than they deserve. It is true that theoretically they appear to be strongly inclined to despotism, but, in actual fact, they prefer equality.

If an Englishman obtains a post in India, he goes there with enthusiasm, and in his imagination pictures the delights that despotism will procure for him. He can, if he likes, keep a harem; he will be surrounded by hundreds of servants — some to keep off the flies which might irritate him, others always ready to carry him in a palanquin. The whole population will crawl before him; he will have the power to order a beating for any Indian who does not obey his wishes with enough zeal or intelligence.

Well, this Englishman who in India wallows in the delights of despotism, hastens to return to England, as soon as he has made his fortune, to enjoy again the advantages of equality. The moment he arrives in harbour in Great Britain he finds himself rudely hustled by the people, and yet that does not make him wish to return to the place where everybody makes way for him.

We see Russians of vast wealth leaving their country to live in western Europe, while western Europeans only go to Russia to make their fortune, and hasten to bring back to their own homes the wealth they have acquired there.

There are good reasons why rich men prefer to live in countries where equality between the members of the community is most far advanced, since these countries are at the same time those where they can most easily and fully satisfy their wants.

In any French town of some importance, a man with money can, at any hour and without previous notice, eat well at a moderate price. In Russia only the great nobles can obtain good food.

If a traveller has a breakdown of his carriage anywhere in England, he can either have his carriage repaired or buy on the spot a carriage as good as the other. In Russia, a traveller whose carriage breaks down on a main road between big towns, is forced to finish his journey in a peasant's cart.

Thus, in fact, the richest and most powerful men have an interest in the growth of equality, since the means of satisfying their wants increases in the same proportion as the levelling of the individuals composing the community.

It is commonly assumed that those who profit by an abuse are strongly attached to it. This is an error; what they are determined on is not to let themselves be deprived of advantages which pass into the hands of others. It was the nobles who in France initiated the suppression of the privileges which they enjoyed, and they regretted this sacrifice only when they saw, first, all the former commoners behave towards them like members of a privileged order, and then a new aristocracy growing up in which the former nobles were only admitted as inferiors.

Let me say what perhaps should have been stated first, that the improvement of the lot of the masses secures the welfare of men of every class, and that, to improve the lot of the masses, it is necessary not merely to transfer privilege, but to abolish it. It is necessary not merely to let abuses change hands, but to eliminate them.

The most direct method of improving the moral and physical welfare of the majority of the population is to give priority in State expenditure to ensuring work for all fit men, to secure their physical existence;

spreading throughout the proletarian class a knowledge of positive science; ensuring for this class forms of recreation and interests which will develop their intelligence.

We must add to this the measures necessary to ensure that the national wealth is administered by men fitted for it, and most concerned in its administration, that is to say the most important industrialists.

Thus the community, by means of these fundamental arrangements, will be organized in a way which will completely satisfy reasonable men of every class.

There will no longer be a fear of insurrection, and consequently no longer a need to maintain large standing armies to suppress it; no longer a need to spend enormous sums on a police force; no longer a fear of foreign danger, for a body of thirty millions of men who are a contented community would easily repel attack, even if the whole human race combined against them.

We might add that neither princes nor peoples would be so mad as to attack a nation of thirty millions who displayed no aggressive intentions against their neighbours, and were united internally by mutual interests.

Furthermore, there would no longer be a need for a system of police-spying in a community in which the vast majority had an interest in maintaining the established order.

The men who brought about the Revolution, the men who directed it, and the men who, since 1789 and up to the present day, have guided the nation, have committed a great political mistake. They have all sought to improve the governmental machine, whereas they should have subordinated it and put administration in the first place.

They should have begun by asking a question the solution of which is simple and obvious. They should have asked who, in the present state of morals and enlightenment, are the men most fitted to manage the affairs of the nation. They would have been forced to recognize the fact that the scientists, artists and industrialists, and the heads of industrial concerns are the men who possess the most eminent, varied, and most positively useful ability, for the guidance of men's minds at the present time. They would have recognized the fact that the work of the scientists, artists, and industrialists is that which, in discovery and application, contributes most to national prosperity.

They would have reached the conclusion that the scientists, artists and leaders of industrial enterprises are the men who should be entrusted with administrative power, that is to say, with the responsibility for managing the national interests; and that the functions of government should be limited to maintaining public order.

The reformers of 1789 should have said to themselves as follows.

The kings of England have given a good example to monarchy by agreeing to give no order without the approval and signature of a minister. The magnanimity of the kings of France demands that they shew still greater generosity to their people, and that they should agree to make no decision affecting the general interests of the nation without the approval of the men most fitted to judge their decisions — that is to say, without the approval of the scientists and the most eminent artists, without the approval of the most important industrialists.

I propose to explain briefly how the imposition of government on top of administration produces harmful effects at the present day, when the mass of the nation consists of men who no longer require to be closely supervised, since they have shewn themselves capable of administering all kinds of property. To-day the proletarian class can only become dangerous to public order, if the administrators of the national interests are so inept or selfish as to let them become unemployed.

It is easy to convince oneself, and others, that one has the capacity to govern, because the ability or lack of ability to govern can only be proved by experience. Any man can imagine and persuade others that he would govern well, so long as he has not governed already.

It is not the same in the case of mathematics, physics, chemistry, physiology, mechanics, poetry, painting, sculpture, architecture, farming, manufacture, commerce, and banking

It is easy for any man to judge whether he possesses great ability in the sciences or arts; it is easy to verify whether he has attained great importance in a branch of industry. In any case, errors of this sort would not be serious, since his neighbours would soon open his eyes, if they were blinded by vanity.

It follows from what I have said that the ambition of scientists, artists and industrialists to participate in the administration of national interests, is not dangerous to the community. It is advantageous rather, since they can only succeed in their ambition through solid achievements; while the ambition which aims at a place in the government is harmful to the community, because the most incapable men may be consumed by such an ambition and, in order to satisfy it, strive to overthrow the whole social order.

One of the important effects of this ambition, which inflamed almost all Frenchmen when the government of the unfortunate Louis XVI was overturned, is very extraordinary. It was with the aim of being governed less, and less expensively, that the nation embarked on revolution. Up to the present it has achieved as a result more government, and more expensive government, than it had before the Revolution.

The industrialists produce much more than before the Revolution, but a great part of the increased production is used to pay useless military staffs, and a mass of clerks who employ their time for the most part in reading newspapers and sharpening pens — a result which satisfies neither the needs nor the feelings of the producers.

The community has often been compared to a pyramid. I admit that the nation would be composed as a pyramid; I am profoundly convinced that the national pyramid should be crowned by the monarchy, but I assert that from the base of the pyramid to its summit the layers should be composed of more and more previous materials. If we consider the present pyramid, it appears that the base is made of granite, that up to a certain height the layers are composed of valuable materials, but that the upper part, supporting a magnificent diamond, is composed of nothing but plaster and gilt.

The base of the present national pyramid consists of workers in their routine occupations; the first layers above this base are the leaders of industrial enterprises, the scientists who improve the methods of manufacture and widen their application, the artists who give the stamp of good taste to all their products. The upper layers, which I assert to be composed of nothing but plaster, which is easily recognizable despite the gilding, are the courtiers, the mass of nobles whether of ancient or recent creation, the idle rich, the governing class from the prime minister to the humblest clerk. The monarchy is the magnificent diamond which crowns the pyramid.

Source: from Henri, Comte de Saint-Simon, *Selected Writings,* ed. and trans. F.M.H. Markham (Basil Blackwell, Oxford, 1952) pp. 72-80.

11 ARISTOCRACY AND THE LOWER CLASSES IN ENGLAND

Alexis de Tocqueville

The English aristocracy has been adroit in more than one respect.

First of all it has always been involved in public affairs; it has taken the initiative in protecting its rights; it has talked a great deal about liberty.

But what distinguishes it from all others is the ease with which it has opened its ranks. It is often said that in England men of all social ranks could rise to important positions. This was, I believe, much less true than was thought: what was taken for a rule, was in fact a rare exception. In general the aristocracy had everything at its disposal. But, with great riches, anybody could hope to enter into the ranks of the aristocracy. Furthermore since everybody could hope to become rich, especially in such a mercantile country as England, a peculiar position arose in that their privileges, which raised such feeling against the aristocrats of other countries, were the thing that most attached the English to theirs. As everybody had the hope of being among the privileged, the privileges made the aristocracy not more hated, but more valued. The reason why the French nobles were the butt of all hatreds, was not chiefly that only the nobles had the right to everything, but because nobody could become a noble. It is this happy combination which made and still makes the power of the aristocracy in England. The English aristocracy in feelings and prejudices resembles all the aristocracies of the world, but it is not in the least founded on birth, that inaccessible thing, but on wealth that everyone can acquire, and this one difference makes it stand, while the others succumb either to the people or to the King.

The aristocracy in England has thus even in our time a power and a force of resistance which it is very difficult for a Frenchman to understand. Those general conceptions which he has formed in his own country or in many others concerning the strength or weakness of aristocracy, must be forgotten here, where he finds himself on entirely new ground.

However the English aristocracy now seems to me to be exposed to dangers to which it will finally succumb.

I remarked earlier that the strength of the English aristocracy did not depend only on itself, but on the feelings of all classes who hope to enter into its ranks. This applied most strongly the nearer a man approached it and so the better were his chances of sharing its privileges. Thus the banker who was a millionaire already and would soon be a great landowner, supported the aristocracy more than did an ordinary London merchant, and the latter more than a shopkeeper, and he in his turn more than a worker.

But in our time the classes who have almost no hope of sharing the privileges of the aristocracy, have become more numerous than they ever were before; they are more enlightened and see more clearly what I have just said. In the classes which have a chance of gaining the privileges of the aristocracy, there is a crowd of people who realise that they can reach this position more quickly by another way. That democratic spirit which in Europe one calls the French spirit, has made startling progress among them.

In any case I believe that the English aristocracy would be in a good position to fight the general difficulties of its present situation, based as it is on the riches and the *instincts* of the nation, if it could provide, as before, material prosperity for the lower classes. For the man of the people to be satisfied in a sphere from which it is almost impossible for him to escape, he must be fairly well-off there. This is more especially true in such a time of intellectual ferment and moral restlessness as ours. But the English people are afflicted by real and profound hardships.

A Frenchman on seeing England for the first time is struck by the apparent comfort and cannot imagine why people complain. But under this brilliant surface are hidden very deep distresses. Moreover one should judge by comparisons here; experience proves that people demand factitious necessities almost as imperiously as natural ones. So it comes about that so many people kill themselves for evils which seem imaginary to their neighbours. In the same way, for the English the lack of certain superfluities to which they have become accustomed by long habit, is as grave as a lack of food or clothing for a Russian. It stirs up in him a feeling of irritation and impatience at least as great.

The aristocracy has thus not only to fight against the difficulties common to all aristocracies in our time, but also against passions aroused by suffering or at least by lack of comfort.

I still persist in believing that if the aristocracy could form a compact body with all the other classes who have some hope of sharing their privileges, it would succeed in holding out, for nothing is more difficult than for a people to make a revolution all by itself.

But that is not how things are. With every increase in the power of democracy the number of people will grow greater who prefer the quicker chances of advancement which it can give, to the more distant ones which the aristocracy offers. Thus up to the present the people enjoy the support of many men whose birth or position should put them on the side of the aristocracy.

Furthermore the first ranks of the nobility have contrived to alienate the second ranks, with the result that the latter no longer support the former as they always did in the past. The fact is that for three years now the House of Lords has seemed isolated in the country. A time will no doubt come when, the danger becoming imminent for the whole aristocracy, the second rank will rally to the first, but by then the revolution will be too far advanced to be stopped.

If any fundamental change in the law, or any social transformation, or any substitution of one regulating principle for another is called a revolution, then England assuredly is in a state of revolution. For the aristocratic principle which was the vital one of the English constitution, is losing strength every day, and it is probable that in due time the democratic one will have taken its place. But if one understands by a revolution a violent and sudden change, then England does not seem ripe for such an event, and I see many reasons for thinking that it will never be so. But I must explain my reasons for thinking this.

In England an illustrious name is a great advantage and a cause of much pride to him who bears it, but in general one can say that the aristocracy is founded on wealth, a thing which may be *acquired*, and not on birth which cannot. From this it results that one can clearly see in England where the aristocracy begins, but it is impossible to say where it ends. It could be compared to the Rhine whose source is to be found on the peak of a high mountain, but which divides into a thousand little streams and, in a manner of speaking, disappears before it reaches the sea. The difference between England and France in this matter turns on the examination of a single word in each language. 'Gentleman' and 'gentilhomme' evidently have the same derivation, but 'gentleman' in England is applied to every well-educated man whatever his birth, while in France *gentilhomme* applies only to a noble by birth. The meaning of these two words of common origin has been so transformed by the different social climates of the two countries that today they simply cannot be translated, at least without recourse to a periphrasis. This grammatical observation is more illuminating than many long arguments.

The English aristocracy can therefore never arouse those violent hatreds felt by the middle and lower classes against the nobility in France where the nobility is an exclusive caste, which while monopolising all privileges and hurting everybody's feelings, offers no hope of ever entering into its ranks.

The English aristocracy has a hand in everything; it is open to everyone; and anyone who wishes to abolish it or attack it as a body, would have a hard task to define the object of his onslaught.

The power of the aristocracy in England, which could be called the domination of the richer classes, is however losing its scope. This is due to several reasons.

The first results from the general movement common to humanity the world over in our time. The century is primarily democratic. Democracy is like a rising tide; it only recoils to come back with greater force, and soon one sees that for all its fluctuations it is always gaining ground. The immediate future of European society is completely democratic; this can in no way be doubted. Thus the common people in England are beginning to get the idea that they, too, can take a part in government. The class placed immediately above it, but which has not yet played a notable part in the course of events, especially shows this ill-defined urge for growth and for power, and is becoming more numerous and more restless day by day. Furthermore the discomforts and real poverty suffered in England in our time, give birth to ideas and excite passions which would perhaps have long continued to sleep if the State had been prosperous.

So a gradual development of the democratic principle must follow from the irresistible march of events. Daily some further privilege of the aristocracy comes under attack; it is a slow war waged about details, but infallibly in time it will bring the whole edifice down.
Moreover the same cause now increases the strength of democracy in England as it once helped to maintain the long domination of the aristocracy; for there is no absolute truth or good in human affairs.

When a body is composed of a limited number of members, clearly defined and exclusively possessing certain privileges, like the nobility in France, such a body makes itself prey to frightful hatreds, but when attacked it defends itself like a single man, all its members having a clear and certain interest in defending the whole body.

Thus at the time of the French Revolution all the nobles took a common line. If the effort had been as well organised as it was great, their resistance might perhaps have been successful.

But in England where the limits of the aristocracy are unknown, there are many of its members who share democratic ideas up to a point, or see advantage to themselves in extending popular power. It thus happens that on many questions the House of Lords is of one opinion, but all the rest of the aristocracy is with the people. On one side there is continual attack, and on the other divided and often weak resistance.

Therefore the English aristocracy will fall more slowly and less violently than the French, but I think that it will fall as inevitably.

These are the general reasons that make me believe that England is not threatened, as is generally believed in France, by a violent and rapid change in its social state.

Now here are the symptoms which I have noted and which, to whatever cause they are attributed, seem to me to show that the revolution which we await is still far away.

When a people has been kept away for centuries from all political activity and in ignorance of everything relating to the government of society, and suddenly the light shines on it, it is impossible to predict what will be the course of its ideas. Some thought which had been barely entertained even by the most heated brain, could become an article of faith for such a people in the course of a single year; and then nothing could be more dangerous than to judge from what people think today what they will think tomorrow.

But that remark is not applicable to England. Freedom of the press has existed in England for more than a century. All questions relating to the government of society, even if they have not been treated in detail, have at least been raised. There is no theory so destructive of the present order that it has not found an echo among those bold spirits who, like the pioneers in America, advance into the wilderness and are often very far ahead of the mass of the people who follow them.

So if the English people are not yet convinced of an idea, one can be sure that it will take some time for them to become so.

It is easy to notice one alarming symptom in England; it is a spirit of innovation spread through all classes, which announces the weakening of the aristocratic principle more than does any other thing. In past times what most distinguished the English people from any other was its satisfaction with itself; then everything about its laws and its customs was good in its eyes. It was drunk in those days with the incense of flattery which it lavished on itself, and sanctified even its prejudices and sorrows. This proud disposition was even further increased by the French writers of the eighteenth century, who all took the English at their word and carried their praises even further than they.

Today everything has changed. In the England of our times a spirit of discontent with the present and hatred of the past shows itself everywhere. The human spirit has fallen into the opposite extreme. It only looks for what is wrong around it, and is much more bent on correcting what is wrong than in preserving what is good.

The English are thus on a dangerous road; but they are taking one small thing after another, and have not in any way conceived one of those general principles which announce the approach of the total subversion of the existing order.

The privileges of the aristocracy are being attacked; it is easy to see that at each step they are losing something of their strength. But it is an indirect attack that is being made against them. Public opinion is far from having taken a stand about the utility of an aristocracy in principle. I even believe that in the present state of opinion the majority are decidedly in favour of the aristocratic principle to a greater or less extent according to the disposition of the individual.

I explained earlier what has made the aristocracy so strong in England. This strength, although it is shaken, is still very great. I was singularly struck during my stay in this country by the extent to which the aristocratic principle affected manners. This is what struck me most in what I say. I think the following notes prove the point completely.

Talk with a man of the people or with a member of the middle classes and you will see that he has a vague feeling of discomfort. He will complain of such-and-such a Lord, or the course which the House of Lords has adopted, but it does not seem to have entered his head that one could do without Lords. His anger will be brought to bear against some individual, but you will only very rarely notice in him that violent feeling, full of hatred and envy, which incites the lower classes in France against all those who are above them. These feelings, it is true, are germinating among the English, but they are not yet developed and perhaps it will be a long time before they are so if the aristocracy avoids a head-on collision with the people.

Listen to the same man on the subject of government; he sees clearly that he should take part in the government, but the idea that government belongs to the people does not strike his imagination.

So, too, if you speak to a member of the middle classes; you will find he hates some aristocrats but not the aristocracy. On the contrary he himself is full of aristocratic prejudices. He deeply distrusts the people; he loves noise, territorial possessions, carriages: he lives in the hope of attaining all this by means of the democratic varnish with which he covers himself, and meanwhile gives a livery to his one servant whom he calls a footman, talks of his dealings with the Duke of — and his very distant family links with the house of another noble Lord.

The whole of English society is still clearly based on an aristocratic footing, and has contracted habits that only a violent revolution or the slow and continual action of new laws can destroy. Luxury and the joys of pride have become necessities of life here. Many still prefer the chance of procuring them in their entirety to the establishment of a universal equality around them in which nothing would come to humiliate them.

... It is not rare to hear an Englishman complain of the extension of aristocratic privileges and to speak with bitterness of those who exploit them; but come to tell him the one way to destroy the aristocracy, which is to change the law of inheritance, and he will draw back at once. I have not yet met one person who did not seem frightened by such an idea. Thus it is true that there is hatred of the aristocrats, but public opinion is far from cold-bloodedly envisaging the destruction of the aristocracy. Moreover, this law of inheritance which is, as it were, the cornerstone of the aristocracy, this law has entered into the customs of all classes. In France the code permits a father to leave one child's share extra to the eldest, but it is very rarely that he does so. In England hardly anyone is obliged by law to make a settlement, but there are few rich men who do not do so; to such an extent has this system of unequal fortunes and the preservation of the family become an accepted habit! Indeed, here as elsewhere, the foundations are unsettled; but the attack is indirect and not open; one thing leads to another without general or defined principles. Each day sees the disappearance of one of the lucrative sinecures which used to go to those younger sons whom their fathers' aristocratic instincts had disinherited. When it will become difficult for younger sons to get anything to live on, the eldest sons will have to divide the inheritance. So here, too, the revolution is on the move, but it goes slowly.

The state of the poor is the deepest trouble of England. The number of paupers is increasing here at an alarming rate, a fact which should to some extent be attributed to the defects of the law. But in my view the first and permanent cause of the evil is the way landed property is not divided up. In England the number of people who possess land is tending to decrease rather than increase, and the number of the proletarians grows ceaselessly with the population. Such conditions tie up with the increase in taxation which means that the rich man cannot employ the poor as he would have been able to, if a large part of his money did not go into the State coffers; such a state of things cannot but indefinitely stimulate poverty. Well then! . . . and what struck me most of all, was that this truth, so far from being generally realised, is not understood except by a few. The thought of even a gradual sharing of the land has not in the least occurred to the public imagination. Some speculators think of it, some agitators seek to exploit it, but to my extreme surprise the masses have not yet got the idea at all. The English are still imbued with that doctrine, which is at least debatable, that great properties are necessary for the improvement of agriculture, and they seem still convinced that extreme inequality of wealth is the natural order of things. Notice that it is not of the rich I am speaking here at all, but of the middle classes and great part of the poor. As long as the imagination of the English has not broken this fetter, and does not follow another chain of ideas, the chances of a violent revolution are few, for, whatever anyone says, it is ideas that stir the world and not blind needs. Certainly when the French Revolution broke out, French imaginations had already gone far beyond these limits.

To sum up, England seems to me in a critical state in that certain events, which it is possible to predict, can from one moment to another throw her into a state of violent revolution. But if things follow their natural course, I do not think that this revolution will come, and I see many chances of the English being able to modify their political and social condition, with much trouble no doubt, but without a convulsion and without civil war.

I have said that a violent revolution was something possible although not probable. In fact when the human spirit begins to move in a people, it is almost impossible to say beforehand where it will end up. Furthermore England, apart from the dangers of Reform, is exposed to other dangers which greatly intensify those; a great financial crisis caused by bankruptcy, an increase in poverty caused by the prolongation of the present Poor Laws coming in the middle of the agitation for Reform, could no doubt give popular passions an impulse which it is very hard to foresee.

But the greatest danger could come from the conduct of the aristocracy. At the moment the House of Lords is isolated in the country and it is very difficult for it efficiently to oppose Reform. But there will come a time when the popular party will gain ground, movement will become more rapid and the final result of the revolution will be clear to all eyes. Then the Lords will find the support they now lack in the country; all the second rank of the aristocracy and all those who have a positive interest in maintaining the old order, will see that they have to make common cause with the high nobility. It is to be feared that the aristocracy may try to oppose the irresistible current of the new ideas. Once the fight is on, it is impossible to say where the winning party will stop, for the English are a violent, although a deliberate, people.

Moreover the blind strength of the lower classes would find a guide in the enlightened ideas of the middle classes, who, at this moment, turn from them in terror and disgust.

Source: from *Journeys to England and Ireland,* trans. George Lawrence and K.P. Mayer (Anchor Books, New York, 1968) pp. 42-5, 51-9.

12 OF PROPERTY AND THE LABOURING CLASSES

John Stuart Mill

The laws and conditions of the production of wealth, partake of the character of physical truths. There is nothing optional, or arbitrary in them. Whatever mankind produce, must be produced in the modes, and under the conditions, imposed by the constitution of external things, and by the inherent properties of their own bodily and mental structure. Whether they like it or not, their productions will be limited by the amount of their previous accumulation, and, that being given, it will be proportional to their energy, their skill, the perfection of their machinery, and their judicious use of the advantages of combined labour. Whether they like it or not, a double quantity of labour will not raise, on the same land, a double quantity of food, unless some improvement takes place in the processes of cultivation. Whether they like it or not, the unproductive expenditure of individuals will *pro tanto* tend to impoverish the community, and only their productive expenditure will enrich it. The opinions, or the wishes, which may exist on these different matters, do not control the things themselves. We cannot, indeed, foresee to what extent the modes of production may be altered, or the productiveness of labour increased, by future extensions of our knowledge of the laws of nature, suggesting new processes of industry of which we have at present no conception. But howsoever we may succeed in making for ourselves more space within the limits set by the constitution of things, we know that there must be limits. We cannot alter the ultimate properties either of matter or mind, but can only employ those properties more or less successfully, to bring about the events in which we are interested.

It is not so with the Distribution of Wealth. That is a matter of human institution solely. The things once there, mankind, individually or collectively, can do with them as they like. They can place them at the disposal of whomsoever they please, and on whatever terms. Further, in the social state, in every state except total solitude, any disposal whatever of them can only take place by the consent of society, or rather of those who dispose of its active force. Even what a person has produced by his individual toil, unaided by any one, he cannot keep, unless by the permission of society. Not only can society take it from him, but individuals could and would take it from him, if society only remained passive; if it did not either interfere *en masse,* or employ and pay people for the purpose of preventing him from being disturbed in the possession. The distribution of wealth, therefore, depends on the laws and customs of society. The rules by which it is determined, are what the opinions and feelings of the ruling portion of the community make them, and are very different in different ages and countries; and might be still more different, if mankind so chose.

The opinions and feelings of mankind, doubtless, are not a matter of chance. They are consequences of the fundamental laws of human nature, combined with the existing state of knowledge and experience, and the existing condition of social institutions and intellectual and moral culture. But the laws of the generation of human opinions are not within our present subject. They are part of the general theory of human progress, a far larger and more difficult subject of inquiry than political economy. We have here to consider, not the causes, but the consequences of the rules according to which wealth may be distributed. Those, at least, are as little arbitrary, and have as much the character of physical laws, as the laws of production. Human beings can control their own acts, but not the consequences of their acts either to themselves or to others. Society can subject the distribution of wealth to whatever rules it thinks best; but what practical results will flow from the operation of those rules, must be discovered, like any other physical or mental truths, by observation and reasoning.

We proceed, then, to the consideration of the different modes of distributing the produce of land and labour, which have been adopted in practice, or may be conceived in theory. Among those, our attention is first claimed by that primary and fundamental institution, on which, unless in some exceptional and very limited cases, the economical arrangements of society have always rested, though in its secondary features it has varied, and is liable to vary. I mean, of course, the institution of individual property.

Private property, as an institution, did not owe its origin to any of those considerations of utility, which plead for the maintenance of it when established. Enough is known of rude ages, both from history and from analogous states of society in our own time, to show, that tribunals (which always precede laws) were originally established, not to determine rights but to repress violence and terminate quarrels. With this object chiefly in view, they naturally enough gave legal effect to first occupancy, by treating as the aggressor the person who first commenced violence, by turning, or attempting to turn, another out of possession. The preservation of the peace, which was the original object of civil government, was thus attained; while by confirming, to those who already possessed it, even what was not the fruit of personal exertion, a guarantee was incidentally given to them and others that they would be protected in what was so.

In considering the institution of property as a question in social philosophy, we must leave out of consideration its actual origin in any of the existing nations of Europe. We may suppose a community unhampered by any previous possession; a body of colonists, occupying for the first time an uninhabited country; bringing nothing with them but what belonged to them in common, and having a clear field for the adoption of the institutions and polity which they judged most expedient; required, therefore, to choose whether they would conduct the work of production on the principle of individual property, or on some system of common ownership and collective agency.

If private property were adopted, we must presume that it would be accompanied by none of the initial inequalities and injustices which obstruct the beneficial operation of the principle in old societies. Every full-grown man or woman, we must suppose, would be secured in the unfettered use and disposal of his or her bodily and mental faculties; and the instruments of production, the land and tools, would be divided fairly among them, so that all might star, in respect to outward appliances, on equal terms. It is possible also to conceive that in this original apportionment, compensation might be made for the injuries of nature, and the balance redressed by assigning to the less robust members of the community advantages in the distribution, sufficient to put them on a par with the rest. But the division, once made, would not again be interfered with; individuals would be left to their own exertions and to the ordinary chances, for making an advantageous use of what was assigned to them. If individual property, on the contrary, were excluded, the plan which must be adopted would be to hold the land and all instruments of production as the joint property of the community, and to carry on the operations of industry on the common account. The direction of the labour of the community would devolve upon a magistrate or magistrates, whom we may suppose elected by the suffrages of the community, and whom we must assume to be voluntarily obeyed by them. The division of the produce would in like manner be a public act. The principle might either be that of complete equality, or of apportionment to the necessities or deserts of individuals, in whatever manner might be conformable to the ideas of justice or policy prevailing in the community.

Examples of such associations, on a small scale, are the monastic orders, the Moravians, the followers of Rapp, and others: and from the hopes which they hold out of relief from the miseries and iniquities of a state of much inequality of wealth, schemes for a larger application of the same idea have reappeared and become popular at all periods of active speculation on the first principles of society. In an age like the present, when a general reconsideration of all first principles is felt to be inevitable, and when more than at any former period of history the suffering portions of the community have a voice in the discussion, it was impossible but that ideas of this nature would spread far and wide. The late revolutions in Europe have thrown up a great amount of speculation of this character, and an unusual share of attention has consequently been drawn to the various forms which these ideas have assumed: nor is this attention likely to diminish, but on the contrary, to increase more and more.

The assailants of the principle of individual property may be divided into two classes: those whose scheme implies absolute equality in the distribution of the physical means of life and enjoyment, and those who admit inequality, but grounded on some principle, or supposed principle, of justice or general expediency, and not, like so many of the existing social inequalities, dependent on accident alone. At the head of the first class, as the earliest of those belonging to the present generation, must be placed Mr. Owen and his followers. M. Louis Blanc and M. Cabet have more recently become conspicuous as apostles of similar doctrines (though the former advocates equality of distribution only as a transition to a still higher standard of justice, that all should work according to their capacity, and receive according to their wants). The characteristic name for this economical system is Communism, a word of continental origin, only of late introduced into this country. The word Socialism, which originated among the English Communists, and was assumed by them as a name to designate their own doctrine, is now, on the Continent, employed in a larger sense; not necessarily implying Communism, or the entire abolition of private property, but applied to any system which requires that the land and the instruments of production should be the property, not of individuals, but of communities or associations, or of the government. Among such systems the two of highest intellectual pretension are those which, from the names of their real or reputed authors, have been called St. Simonism and Fourierism; the former, defunct as a system, but which during the few years of its public promulgation, sowed the seeds of nearly all the Socialist tendencies which have since spread so widely in France: the second, still flourishing in the number, talent, and zeal of its adherents.

The observations in the preceding chapter had for their principal object to deprecate a false ideal of human society. Their applicability to the practical purposes of present times, consists in moderating the inordinate importance attached to the mere increase of production, and fixing attention upon improved distribution, and a large remuneration of labour, as the two desiderata. Whether the aggregate produce increases absolutely or not, is a thing in which, after a certain amount has been obtained, neither the legislator nor the philanthropist need feel any strong interest: but, that it should increase relatively to the number of those who share in it, is of the utmost possible importance; and this, (whether the wealth of mankind be stationary, or increasing at the most rapid rate ever known in an old country), must depend on the opinions and habits of the most numerous class, the class of manual labourers.

When I speak, either in this place or elsewhere, of 'the labouring classes', or of labourers as a 'class', I use those phrases in compliance with custom, and as descriptive of an existing, but by no means a necessary or permanent state of social relations. I do not recognise as either just or salutary, a state of society in which there is any 'class' which is not labouring; any human beings, exempt from bearing their share of the necessary labours of human life, except those unable to labour or who have fairly earned rest by previous toil. So long, however, as the great social evil exists of a non-labouring class, labourers also constitute a class, and may be spoken of, though only provisionally, in that character.

Considered in its moral and social aspect, the state of the labouring people has latterly been a subject of much more speculation and discussion than formerly; and the opinion, that it is not now what it ought to be, has become very general. The suggestions which have been promulgated, and the controversies which have been excited, on detached points rather than on the foundations of the subject, have put in evidence the existence of two conflicting theories, respecting the social position desirable for manual labourers. The one may be called the theory of dependence and protection, the other that of self-dependence.

According to the former theory, the lot of the poor, in all things which affect them collectively, should be regulated *for* them, not *by* them. They should not be required or encouraged to think for themselves, or give to their own reflection or forecast an influential voice in the determination of their destiny. It is supposed to be the duty of the higher classes to think for them, and to take the responsibility of their lot, as the commander and officers of an army take that of the soldiers composing it. This function, it is contended, the higher classes should prepare themselves to perform conscientiously, and their whole demeanour should impress the poor with a reliance on it, in order that, while yielding passive and active obedience to the rules prescribed for them, they may resign themselves in all other respects to a trustful *insouciance,* and repose under the shadow of their protectors. The relation between rich and poor, according to this theory, (a theory also applied to the relation between men and women) should be amiable, moral, and sentimental: affectionate tutelage on the one side, respectful and grateful deference on the other. The rich should be *in loco parentis* to the poor, guiding and restraining them like children. Of spontaneous action on their part there should be no need. They should be called on for nothing but to do their day's work, and to be moral and religious. Their morality and religion should be provided for them by their superiors, who should see them properly taught it, and should do all that is necessary to ensure their being, in return for labour and attachment, properly fed, clothed, housed, spiritually edified, and innocently amused.

This is the ideal of the future, in the minds of those whose dissatisfaction with the Present assumes the form of affection and regret towards the Past. Like other ideals, it exercises an unconscious influence on the opinions and sentiments of numbers who never consciously guide themselves by any ideal. It has also this in common with other ideals, that it has never been historically realized. It makes its appeal to our imaginative sympathies in the character of a restoration of the good times of our forefathers. But no times can be pointed out in which the higher classes of this or any other country performed a part even distantly resembling the one assigned to them in this theory. It is an idealization, grounded on the conduct and character of here and there an individual. All privileged and powerful classes, as such, have used their power in the interest of their own selfishness, and have indulged their self-importance in despising, and not in lovingly caring for, those who were, in their estimation, degraded, by being under the necessity of working for their benefit. I do not affirm that what has always been must always be, or that human improvement has no tendency to correct the intensely selfish feelings engendered by power; but though the evil may be lessened, it cannot be eradicated, until the power itself is withdrawn. This, at least, seems to me undeniable, that long before the superior classes could be sufficiently improved to govern in the tutelary manner supposed, the inferior classes would be too much improved to be so governed.

I am quite sensible of all that is seductive in the picture of society which this theory presents. Though the facts of it have no prototype in the past, the feelings have. In them lies all that there is of reality in the conception. As the idea is essentially repulsive of a society only held together by the relations and feelings arising out of pecuniary interests, so there is something naturally attractive in a form of society abounding in strong personal attachments and disinterested self-devotion. Of such feelings it must be admitted that the relation of protector and protected has hitherto been the richest source. The strongest attachments of human beings in general, are towards the things or the persons that stand between them and some dreaded evil. Hence, in an age of lawless violence and insecurity, and general hardness and roughness of manners, in which life is beset with dangers and sufferings at every step, to those who have neither a commanding position of their own, nor a claim on the protection of some one who has — a generous giving of protection, and a grateful receiving of it, are the strongest ties which connect human beings; the feelings arising from that relation are their warmest feelings; all the enthusiasm and tenderness of the most sensitive natures gather round it; loyalty on the one part and chivalry on the other are principles exalted into passions. I do not desire to depreciate these qualities. The error lies in not perceiving, that these virtues and sentiments, like the clanship and the hospitality of the wandering Arab, belong emphatically to a rude and imperfect state of the social union, and that the feelings between protector and protected, whether between kings and subjects, rich and poor, or men and women, can no longer have this beautiful and endearing character, where there are no longer any serious dangers from which to protect. What is there in the present state of society to make it natural that human beings of ordinary strength and courage, should glow with the warmest gratitude and devotion in return for protection? The laws protect them; wherever the laws do not criminally fail in their duty. To be under the power of some one, instead of being as formerly the sole condition of safety, is now, speaking generally, the only situation which exposes to grievous wrong. The so-called protectors are now the only persons against whom, in any ordinary circumstances, protection is needed. The brutality and tyranny with which every police report is filled, are those of husbands to wives, of parents to children. That the law does not prevent these atrocities, that it is only now making a first timid attempt to repress and punish them, is no matter of necessity, but the deep disgrace of those by whom the laws are made and administered. No man or woman who either possesses or is able to earn an independent livelihood requires any other protection than that which the law could and ought to give. This being the case, it argues great ignorance of human nature to continue taking for granted that relations founded on protection must always subsist, and not to see that the assumption of the part of protector, and of the power which belongs to it, without any of the necessities which justify it, must engender feelings opposite to loyalty.

Of the working men, at least in the more advanced countries of Europe, it may be pronounced certain, that the patriarchal or paternal system of government is one to which they will not again be subject. That question was decided, when they were taught to read, and allowed access to newspapers and political tracts; when dissenting preachers were suffered to go among them, and appeal to their faculties and feelings in opposition to the creeds professed and countenanced by their superiors; when they were brought together in numbers, to work socially under the same roof; when railways enabled them to shift from place to place, and change their patrons and employers as easily as their coats; when they were encouraged to seek a share in the government, by means of the electoral franchise. The working classes have taken their interests into their own hands, and are perpetually showing that they think the interests of their employers not identical with their own, but opposite to them. Some among the higher classes flatter themselves that these tendencies may be counteracted by moral and religious education; but they have let the time go by for giving an education which can serve their purpose. The principles of the Reformation have reached as low down in society as reading and writing, and the poor will not much longer accept morals and religion of other people's prescribing. I speak more particularly of this country, especially the town population, and the districts of the most scientific agriculture or the highest wages, Scotland and the north of England. Among the more inert and less modernized agricultural population of the southern counties, it might be possible for the gentry to retain, for some time longer, something of the ancient deference and submission of the poor, by bribing them with high wages and constant employment; by ensuring them support, and never requiring them to do anything which they do not like. But these are two conditions which never have been combined, and never can be, for long together. A guarantee of subsistence can only be practically kept up, when work is enforced, and superfluous multiplication restrained, by at least a moral compulsion. It is then, that the would-be revivers of old times which they do not understand, would feel practically in how hopeless a task they were engaged. The whole fabric of patriarchal or seignorial influence, attempted to be raised on the foundation of caressing the poor, would be shattered against the necessity of enforcing a stringent Poor-law.

It is on a far other basis that the well-being and well-doing of the labouring people must henceforth rest. The poor have come out of leading-strings, and cannot any longer be governed or treated like children. To their own qualities must now be commended the care of their destiny. Modern nations will have to learn the lesson, that the well-being of a people must exist by means of the justice and self-government. . . . of the individual citizens. The theory of dependence attempts to dispense with the necessity of these qualities in the dependent classes. But now, when even in position they are becoming less and less dependent, and their minds less and less acquiescent in the degree of dependence which remains, the virtues of independence are those which they stand in need of. Whatever advice, exhortation, or guidance is held out to the labouring classes, must henceforth be tendered to them as equals, and accepted by them with their eyes open. The prospect of the future depends on the degree in which they can be made rational beings.

There is no reason to believe that prospect other than hopeful. The progress indeed has hitherto been, and still is slow. But there is a spontaneous education going on in the minds of the multitude, which may be greatly accelerated and improved by artificial aids. The instruction obtained from newspapers and political tracts may not be the most solid kind of instruction, but it is an immense improvement upon none at all. What it does for a people, has been admirably exemplified during the cotton crisis, in the case of the Lancashire spinners and weavers; who have acted with the consistent good sense and forbearance so justly applauded, simply because, being readers of newspapers, they understood the causes of the calamity which had befallen them, and knew that it was in no way imputable either to their employers or to the Government. It is not certain that their conduct would have been as rational and exemplary, if the distress had preceded the salutary measure of fiscal emancipation which gave existence to the penny press. The institutions for lectures and discussion, the collective deliberations on questions of common interest, the trades unions, the political agitation, all serve to awaken public spirit, to diffuse variety of ideas among the mass, and to excite thought and reflection in the more intelligent. Although the too early attainment of political franchises by the least educated class might retard, instead of promoting, their improvement, there can be little doubt that it has been greatly stimulated by the attempt to acquire them. In the meantime, the working classes are now part of the public; in all discussions on matters of general interest they, or a portion of them, are now partakers; all who use the press as an instrument may, if it so happens, have them for an audience; the avenues of instruction through which the middle classes acquire such ideas as they have, are accessible to, at least, the operatives in the towns. With these resources, it cannot be doubted that they will increase in intelligence, even by their own unaided efforts; while there is reason to hope that great improvements both in the quality and quantity of school education will be effected by the exertions either of Government or of individuals, and that the progress of the mass of the people in mental cultivation, and in the virtues which are dependent on it, will take place more rapidly, and with fewer intermittences and aberrations, than if left to itself.

From this increase of intelligence, several effects may be confidently anticipated. First: that they will become even less willing than at present to be led and governed, and directed into the way they should go, by the mere authority and *prestige* of superiors. If they have not now, still less will they have hereafter, any deferential awe, or religious principle of obedience, holding them in mental subjection to a class above them. The theory of dependence and protection will be more and more intolerable to them, and they will require that their conduct and condition shall be essentially self-governed. It is, at the same time, quite possible that they may demand, in many cases, the intervention of the legislature in their affairs, and the regulation by law of various things which concern them, often under very mistaken ideas of their interest. Still, it is their own will, their own ideas and suggestions, to which they will demand that effect should be given, and not rules laid down for them by other people. It is quite consistent with this, that they should feel respect for superiority of intellect and knowledge, and defer much to the opinions, on any subject, of those whom they think well acquainted with it. Such deference is deeply grounded in human nature; but they will judge for themselves of the persons who are and are not entitled to it.

It appears to me impossible but that the increase of intelligence, of education, and of the love of independence among the working classes, must be attended with a corresponding growth of the good sense which manifests itself in provident habits of conduct, and that population, therefore, will bear a gradually diminishing ratio to capital and employment. This most desirable result would be much accelerated by another change, which lies in the direct line of the best tendencies of the time; the opening of industrial occupations freely to both sexes. The same reasons which make it no longer necessary that the poor should depend on the rich, make it equally unnecessary that women should depend on men, and the least which justice requires is that law and custom should not enforce dependence (when the correlative protection has become superfluous) by ordaining that a woman, who does not happen to have a provision by inheritance, shall have scarcely any means open to her of gaining a livelihood, except as a wife and mother. Let women who prefer that occupation, adopt it; but that there should be no option, no other career possible for the great majority of women, except in the humbler departments of life, is a flagrant social injustice. The ideas and institutions by which the accident of sex is made the groundwork of an inequality of legal rights and a forced dissimilarity of social functions, must ere long be recognised as the greatest hindrance to moral, social, and even intellectual improvement. On the present occasion I shall only indicate, among the probable consequences of the industrial and social independence of women, a great diminution of the evil of over-population. It is by devoting one-half of the human species to that exclusive function, by making it fill the entire life of one sex, and interweave itself with almost all the objects of the other, that the animal instinct in question is nursed into the disproportionate preponderance which it has hitherto exercised in human life.

The political consequences of the increasing power and importance of the operative classes, and of the growing ascendancy of numbers, which even in England and under the present institutions, is rapidly giving to the will of the majority at least a negative voice in the acts of government, are too wide a subject to be discussed in this place. But, confining ourselves to economical considerations, and notwithstanding the effect which improved intelligence in the working classes, together with just laws, may have in altering the distribution of the produce to their advantage, I cannot think that they will be permanently contented with the condition of labouring for wages as their ultimate state. They may be willing to pass through the class of servants in their way to that of employers; but not to remain in it all their lives. To begin as hired labourers, then after a few years to work on their own account, and finally employ others, is the normal condition of labourers in a new country, rapidly increasing in wealth and population, like America or Australia. But in an old and fully peopled country, those who begin life as labourers for hire, as a general rule, continue such to the end, unless they sink into the still lower grade of recipients of public charity. In the present stage of human progress, when ideas of equality are daily spreading more widely among the poorer classes, and can no longer be checked by anything short of the entire suppression of printed discussion and even of freedom of speech, it is not to be expected that the division of the human race into two hereditary classes, employers and employed, can be permanently maintained. The relation is nearly as unsatisfactory to the payer of wages as to the receiver. If the rich regard the poor as, by a kind of natural law, their servants and dependents, the rich in their turn are regarded as a mere prey and pasture for the poor; the subject of demands and expectations wholly indefinite, increasing in extent with every concession made to them. The total absence of regard for justice or fairness in the relations between the two, is as marked on the side of the employed as on that of the employers. We look in vain among the working classes in general for the just pride which will choose to give good work for good wages: for the most part, their sole endeavour is to receive as much, and return as little in the shape of service, as possible. It will sooner or later become insupportable to the employing classes to live in close and hourly contact with persons whose interests and feelings are in hostility to them. Capitalists are almost as much interested as labourers, in placing the operations of industry on such a footing, that those who labour for them may feel the same interest in the work, which is felt by those who labour on their own account.

The opinion expressed in a former part of this treatise respecting small landed properties and peasant proprietors, may have made the reader anticipate that a wide diffusion of property in land is the resource on which I rely for exempting at least the agricultural labourers from exclusive dependence on labour for hire. Such, however, is not my opinion. I indeed deem that form of agricultural economy to be most groundlessly cried down, and to be greatly preferable, in its aggregate effects on human happiness, to hired labour in any form in which it exists at present; because the prudential check to population acts more directly, and is shown by experience to be more efficacious; and because, in point of security, of independence, of exercise for any other than the animal faculties, the state of a peasant proprietor is far superior to that of an agricultural labourer in this or in any other old country. Where the former system already exists, and works on the whole satisfactorily, I should regret, in the present state of human intelligence, to see it abolished in order to make way for the other, under a pedantic notion of agricultural improvement as a thing necessarily the same in every diversity of circumstances. In a backward state of industrial improvement, as in Ireland, I should urge its introduction, in preference to an exclusive system of hired labour; as a more powerful instrument for raising a population from semi-savage listlessness and recklessness, to persevering industry and prudent calculation.

But a people who have once adopted the large system of production, either in manufacturers or in agriculture, are not likely to recede from it; and when population is kept in due proportion to the means of support, it is not desirable that they should. Labour is unquestionably more productive on the system of large industrial enterprises; the produce, if not greater absolutely, is greater in proportion to the labour employed: the same number of persons can be supported equally well with less toil and greater leisure; which will be wholly an advantage, as soon as civilization and improvement have so far advanced, that what is a benefit to the whole shall be a benefit to each individual composing it. And in the moral aspect of the question, which is still more important than the economical, something better should be aimed at as the goal of industrial improvement, than to disperse mankind over the earth in single families, each ruled internally, as families now are, by a patriarchal despot, and having scarcely any community of interest, or necessary mental communion, with other human beings. The domination of the head of the family over the other members, in this state of things, is absolute; while the effect on his own mind tends towards concentration of all interests in the family, considered as an expansion of self, and absorption of all passions in that of exclusive possession, of all cares in those of preservation and acquisition. As a step out of the merely animal state into the human, out of reckless abandonment to brute instincts into prudential foresight and self-government, this moral condition may be seen without displeasure. But if public spirit, generous sentiments, or true justice and equality are desired, association, not isolation, of interests, is the school in which these excellences are nurtured. The aim of improvement should be not solely to place human beings in a condition in which they will be able to do without one another, but to enable them to work with or for one another in relations not involving dependence. Hitherto there has been no alternative for those who lived by their labour, but that of labouring either each for himself alone, or for a master. But the civilizing and improving influences of association, and the efficiency and economy of production on a large scale, may be obtained without dividing the producers into two parties with hostile interests and feelings, the many who do the work being mere servants under the command of the one who supplies the funds, and having no interest of their own in the enterprise except to earn their wages with as little labour as possible. The speculations and discussions of the last fifty years, and the events of the last twenty, are abundantly conclusive on this point. If the improvement which even triumphant military despotism has only retarded, not stopped, shall continue its course, there can be little doubt that the *status* of hired labourers will gradually tend to confine itself to the description of workpeople whose low moral qualities render them unfit for anything more independent: and that the relation of masters and workpeople will be gradually superseded by partnership, in one of two forms: in some cases, association of the labourers with the capitalist; in others, and perhaps finally in all, association of labourers among themselves.

Source: from *Principles of Political Economy* (Longman Green, London, 1865) pp. 123-5, 455-61.

13 OBEISANCES, TITLES AND CLASS DISTINCTIONS

Herbert Spencer

If, in primitive states, men are honoured according to their prowess — if their prowess is estimated here by the number of heads they can show, there by the number of jaw-bones, and elsewhere by the number of scalps — if such trophies are treasured up for generations and the pride of families is proportioned to the number of them taken by ancestors — if of the Gauls in the time of Posidonius, we read that 'the heads of their enemies that were the chiefest persons of quality, they carefully deposit in chests, embalming them with the oil of cedars, showing them to strangers, glory and boast' that they or their forefathers had refused great sums of money for them; then, obviously, a kind of class distinction is initiated by trophies. On reading that in some places a man's rank varies with the quantity of bones in or upon his dwelling, we cannot deny that the display of these proofs of personal superiority, originates a regulative influence in social intercourse.

As political control evolves, trophy-taking becomes in several ways instrumental to the maintenance of authority. Beyond the awe felt for the chief whose many trophies show his powers of destruction, there comes the greater awe which, on growing into a king with subordinate chiefs and dependent tribes, he excites by accumulating the trophies others take on his behalf; rising into dread when he exhibits in numbers the relics of slain rulers. As the practice assumes this developed form, the receipt of such vicariously-taken trophies passes into a political ceremony. The heap of hands laid before an ancient Egyptian king, served to propitiate; as now serves the mass of jawbones sent by an Ashantee captain to the court. When we read of Timour's soldiers that 'their cruelty was enforced by the peremptory command of producing an adequate number of heads', we are conclusively shown that the presentation of trophies hardens into a form expressing obedience. Nor is it thus only that a political effect results. There is the governmental restraint produced by fixing up the bodies or heads of the insubordinate and the felonious. ...

The chief significance of trophy-taking, however, has yet to be pointed out. The reason for here dealing with it, though in itself scarcely to be classed as a ceremony, is that it furnishes us with the key to numerous ceremonies prevailing all over the world among the uncivilized and semi-civilized. From the practice of cutting off and taking away portions of the dead body, there grows up the practice of cutting off portions of the living body.

MUTILATIONS

... This giving a part instead of giving the whole, where the whole cannot be mechanically handed over, will perhaps be instanced as a symbolic ceremony; though, even in the absence of any further interpretation, we may say that it approaches as nearly to actual transfer as the nature of the case permits. We are not, however, obliged to regard this ceremony as artificially devised. We may affiliate it upon a simpler ceremony which at once elucidates it, and is elucidated by it. I refer to surrendering a part of the body as implying surrender of the whole. In Fiji, tributaries approaching their masters were told by a messenger 'that they must all cut off their *tobe* (locks of hair that are left like tails). They all docked their tails.' Still, it may be replied that this act, too, is a symbolic act – an act artificially devised rather than naturally derived. If we carry our inquiry a step back, however, we shall find a clue to its natural derivation.

First, let us remember the honour which accrues from accumulated trophies; so that, among the Shoshones for instance, 'he who takes the most scalps gains the most glory'. Let us join with this Bancroft's statement respecting the treatment of prisoners by the Chichimecs, that 'often were they scalped while yet alive, and the bloody trophy placed upon the heads of their tormentors'. And then let us ask what happens if the scalped enemy survives. The captor preserves the scalp as an addition to his other trophies; the vanquished enemy becomes his slave; and he is shown to be a slave by the loss of his scalp. Here, then, are the beginnings of a custom that may become established when social conditions make it advantageous to keep conquered foes as servants instead of eating them. The conservative savage changes as little as possible. While the new practice of enslaving the captured arises, the old practice of cutting from their bodies such parts as serve for trophies continues; and the marks left become marks of subjugation. Gradually as the receipt of such marks comes to imply bondage, not only will those taken in war be marked, but also those born to them; until at length the bearing of the mark shows subordination in general.

That submission to mutilation may eventually grow into the sealing of an agreement to be bondsmen, is shown us by Hebrew history. 'Then Nahash the Ammonite came up, and encamped against Jabesh-gilead: and all the men of Jabesh said unto Nahash, Make a covenant with us, and we will serve thee. And Nahash the Ammonite answered them, On this condition will I make a covenant with you, that I may thrust out all your right eyes.' They agreed to become subjects, and the mutilation (not in this case consented to, however) was to mark their subjection. And while mutilations thus serve, like the brands a farmer puts on his sheep, to show first private ownership and afterwards political ownership, they also serve as perpetual reminders of the ruler's power: so keeping alive the dread that brings obedience. This fact we see in the statement that when the second Basil deprived fifteen thousand Bulgarian captives of sight, 'the nation was awed by this terrible example'. ...

Prompted by his belief that the spirit pervades the corpse, the savage preserves relics of dead enemies partly in the expectation that he will be enabled thereby to coerce their ghosts — if not himself, still by the help of the medicine-man. He has a parallel reason for preserving a part cut from one whom he has enslaved: both he and the slave think that he so obtains a power to inflict injury. Remembering that the sorcerer's first step is to procure some hair or nail-parings of his victim, or else some piece of his dress pervaded by that odour which is identified with his spirit; it appears to be a necessary corollary that the master who keeps by him a slave's tooth, a joint from his little finger, or even a lock of his hair, thereby retains a power of delivering him over to the sorcerer, who may bring on him one or other fearful evil — torture by demons, disease, death. ...

The evidence that mutilation of the living has been a sequence of trophy-taking from the slain, is thus abundant and varied. Taking the trophy implies victory carried to the death; and the derived practice of cutting off a part from a prisoner implies subjugation of him. Eventually the voluntary surrender of such a part expresses submission; and becomes a propitiatory ceremony because it does this.

Hands are cut off from dead enemies; and, answering to this, besides some identical mutilations of criminals, we have the cutting off of fingers or portions of fingers, to pacify living chiefs, deceased persons, and gods. Noses are among the trophies taken from slain foes; and we have loss of noses inflicted on captives, on slaves, on transgressors of certain kinds. Ears are brought back from the battle-field; and occasionally they are cut off from prisoners, felons, or slaves; while there are peoples among whom pierced ears mark the servant or the subject. Jaws and teeth, too, are trophies; and teeth, in some cases knocked out in propitiation of a dead chief, are, in various other cases, knocked out by a priest as a quasi-religious ceremony. Scalps are taken from killed enemies, and sometimes their hair is used to decorate a victor's dress; and then come various sequences. Here the enslaved have their heads cropped; here scalp-locks are worn subject to a chief's ownership, and occasionally demanded in sign of submission; while, elsewhere, men sacrifice their beards to their rulers: unshorn hair being thus rendered a mark of rank. Among numerous peoples, hair is sacrificed to propitiate the ghosts of relatives; whole tribes cut it off on the deaths of their chiefs or kings; and it is yielded up to express subjection to deities. Occasionally it is offered to a living superior in token of respect; and this complimentary offering is extended to others. Similarly with genital mutilations: there is a like taking of certain parts from slain enemies and from living prisoners; and there is a presentation of them to kings and to gods. Self-bleeding, initiated partly, perhaps, by cannibalism, but more extensively by the mutual giving of blood in pledge of loyalty, enters into several ceremonies expressing subordination: we find it occurring in propitiation of ghosts and of gods, and occasionally as a compliment to living persons. Naturally it is the same with the resulting marks. Originally indefinite in form and place but rendered definite by custom, and at length often decorative, these healed wounds, at first entailed only on relatives of deceased persons, then on all the followers of a man much feared while alive, so become marks expressive of subjection to a dead ruler, and eventually to a god: growing thus into tribal and national marks.

If, as we have seen, trophy-taking as a sequence of conquest enters as a factor into those governmental restraints which conquest initiates, it is to be inferred that the mutilations originated by trophy-taking will do the like. The evidence justifies this inference. Beginning as marks of personal slavery and becoming marks of political and religious subordination, they play a part like that of oaths of fealty and pious self-dedications. Moreover, being acknowledgements of submission to a ruler, visible or invisible, they enforce authority by making conspicuous the extent of his sway. And where they signify class-subjection, as well as where they show the subjugation of criminals, they further strengthen the regulative agency.

OBEISANCES

Concerning a party of Shoshones surprised by them, Lewis and Clarke write — 'The other two, an elderly woman and a little girl, seeing we were too near for them to escape, sat on the ground, and holding down their heads seemed as if reconciled to the death which they supposed awaited them. The same habit of holding down the head and inviting the enemy to strike, when all chance of escape is gone, is preserved in Egypt to this day.' Here we are shown an effort to propitiate by absolute submission; and from acts so prompted originate obeisances.

When, at the outset, in illustration of the truth that ceremony precedes not only social evolution but human evolution, I named the behaviour of a small dog which throws itself on its back in presence of an alarming great dog, probably many readers thought I was putting on this behaviour a forced construction. They would not have thought so had they known that a parallel mode of behaviour occurs among human beings. Livingstone says of the Batoka salutation – 'they throw themselves on their backs on the ground, and, rolling from side to side, slap the outside of their thighs as expressions of thankfulness and welcome.' The assumption of this attitude, which implies – 'You need not subdue me, I am subdued already', is the best means of obtaining safety. Resistance arouses the destructive instincts; and prostration on the back negatives resistance. Another attitude equally helpless, more elaborately displays subjugation. 'At Tonga Tabu . . . the common people show their great chief . . . the greatest respect imaginable by prostrating themselves before him, and by putting his foot on their necks.' The like occurs in Africa. Laird says the messengers from the king of Fundah 'each bent down and put my foot on their heads'. And among historic peoples this position, originated by defeat, became a position assumed in acknowledging submission.

From such primary obeisances representing completely the attitudes of the conquered beneath the conqueror, there come obeisances which express in various ways the subjection of the slave to the master. Of old in the East this subjection was expressed when 'Ben-hadad's servants girded sackcloth on their loins, and put ropes on their heads, and came to the king of Israel'. In Peru, where the militant type of organization was pushed so far, a sign of humility was to have the hands tied and a rope round the neck. In both cases there was an assumption of those bonds which originally marked captives brought from the battle-field. Along with this mode of simulating slavery to the Ynca, another mode was employed. Servitude had to be indicated by carrying a burden; and 'this taking up a load to enter the presence of Atahuallpa, is a ceremony which was performed by all the lords who have reigned in that land'.

These extreme instances I give at the outset by way of showing the natural genesis of the obeisance as a means of obtaining mercy; first from a victor and then from a ruler. A full conception of the obeisance, however, includes another element. In the introductory chapter it was pointed out that sundry signs of pleasure, having a physio-psychological origin, which occur in presence of those for whom there is affection, pass into complimentary observances; because men are pleased by supposing themselves liked, and are therefore pleased by demonstrations of liking. So that while trying to propitiate a superior by expressing submission to him, there is generally an endeavour further to propitiate him by showing joy at his presence. Keeping in view both these elements of the obeisance, let us now consider its varieties; with their political, religious, and social uses.

Though the loss of power to resist which prostration on the face implies, does not reach the utter defencelessness implied by prostration on the back, yet it is great enough to make it a sign of profound homage; and hence it occurs as an obeisance wherever despotism is unmitigated and subordination slavish. In ancient America, before a Chibeha cazique, 'people had to appear prostrate and wish their faces touching the ground'. In Africa, 'when he addresses the king, a Borghoo man stretches himself on the earth as flat as a flounder.' Asia furnishes many instances. 'When preferring a complaint, a Khond or Panoo will throw himself on his face with his hands joined', and while, in Siam, 'before the nobles all subordinates are in a state of reverent prostration, the nobles themselves, in the presence of the sovereign, exhibit the same crawling obeisance'. Similarly in Polynesia. Falling on the face was a mark of submission among the Sandwich Islanders: the king did so to Cook when he first met him. And in the records of ancient historic peoples kindred illustrations are given; as when Mephibosheth fell on his face and did reverence before David; or as when the king of Bithynia fell on his face before the Roman senate. In some cases this attitude of the conquered before the conqueror, has its meaning emphasized by repetition. Bootan supplies an instance; 'They made before the Raja nine prostrations, which is the obeisance paid to him by his subjects whenever they are permitted to approach.'

Every kind of ceremony is apt to have its primitive character obscured by abridgment; and by abridgment this profoundest of obeisances is rendered a less profound one. In performing a full-length prostration there is passed through an attitude in which the body is on the knees with the head on the ground; and to rise, it is needful to draw up the knees before raising the head and getting on the feet. Hence this attitude may be considered as an incomplete prostration. It is a very general one. Among the Coast Negroes, if a native 'goes to visit his superior, or meets him by chance, he immediately falls on his knees, and thrice successively kisses the earth'. In acknowledgment of his inferiority, the king of the Brass people never spoke to the king of the Ibos 'without going down on his knees and touching the ground with his head'. At Embomma, on the Congo, 'the mode of salutation is by gently clapping the hands, and an inferior at the same time goes on his knees and kisses the bracelet on the superior's ancle'.

Often the humility of this obeisance is increased by emphasizing the contact with the earth. On the lower Niger, 'as a mark of great respect, men prostrate themselves, and strike their heads against the ground'. When, in past ages, the Emperor of Russia was crowned, the nobility did homage by 'bending down their heads, and knocking them at his feet to the very ground'. In China at the present time, among the eight kinds of obeisances, increasing in humility, the fifth is kneeling and striking the head on the ground; the sixth, kneeling and thrice knocking the head, which again doubled makes the seventh, and trebled the eighth: this last being due to the Emperor and to Heaven. Among the Hebrews, repetition had a kindred meaning. 'Jacob bowed himself to the ground seven times, until he came near to his brother.'

Naturally this attitude of the conquered man, used by the slave before his master and the subject before his ruler, becomes that of the worshipper before his deity. We find complete prostrations made whether the being to be propitiated is visible or invisible. 'Abraham fell upon his face' before God when he covenanted with him; 'Nebuchadnezzar fell upon his face and worshipped Daniel'; and when Nebuchadnezzar set up a golden image there was a threat of death on 'whoso falleth not down and worshippeth'. Similarly, the incomplete prostration in presence of kings recurs in presence of deities. When making obeisances to their idols, the Mongols touch the ground with the forehead. The Japanese in their temples 'fall down upon their knees, bow their head quite to the ground, slowly and with great humility'. And sketches of Mahommedans at their devotions familiarize us with a like attitude.

From the positions of prostration on back or face, and of semi-prostration on knees, we pass to sundry others; which, however, continue to imply relative inability to resist. In some cases it is permissible to vary the attitude, as in Dahomey, where 'the highest officers lie before the king in the position of Romans upon the *triclinium*. At times they roll over upon their bellies, or relieve themselves by standing "on all fours". Duran states that 'cowering was, with the Mexicans, the posture of respect, as with us is genuflexion'. Crouching shows homage among the New Caledonians; as it does in Fiji, and in Tahiti.

Other changes in attitudes of this class are entailed by the necessities of locomotion. In Dahomey 'when approaching royalty their either crawl like snakes or shuffle forward on their knees'. When changing their places before a superior, the Siamese 'drag themselves on their hands and knees'. In Java an inferior must 'walk with his hams upon his heels until he is out of his superior's sight'. Similarly with the subjects of a Zulu king — even with his wives. And in Loango, extension of this attitude to the household appears not to be limited to the court: wives in general 'dare not speak to them (their husbands) but upon their bare knees, and in meeting them must creep upon their hands'. A neighbouring state furnishes an instance of gradation in these forms of partial prostration; and a recognized meaning in the gradation. The Dakro, a woman who bears messages from the Dahoman King to the Meu, goes on all four before the king; and 'as a rule she goes on all fours to the Meu, and only kneels to smaller men, who become quadrupeds to her'.

Here we come, incidentally, upon a further abridgment of the original prostration; whence results one of the most widely-spread obeisances. As from the entirely prone posture we pass to the posture of the Mahommedan worshipper with forehead on the ground; so from this we pass to the posture on all fours, and from this, by raising the body, to simple kneeling. That kneeling is, and has been in countless places and times, a form of political homage, a form of domestic homage, and a form of religious homage, needs no showing. We will note only that it is, and has been, in all cases associated with coercive government; as in Africa, where 'by thus constantly practising genuflexion upon the hard ground, their [the Dahomans'] knees in time become almost as hard as their heels'. as in Japan, where 'on leaving the presence of the Emperor, officers walk backwards on their knees', as in China, 'where the Viceroy's children as they passed by their father's tent, fell on their knees and bowed three times, with their faces towards the ground', and as in mediæval Europe, where serfs knelt to their masters and feudal vassals to their suzerains.

Not dwelling on the transition from descent on both knees to descent on one knee, which, less abject, comes a stage nearer the erect attitude, it will suffice to note the transition from kneeling on one knee to bending the knee. That this form of obeisance is an abridgment, is well shown us by the Japanese.

> On meeting, they show respect by bending the knee; and when they wish to do unusual honour to an individual they place themselves on the knee and bow down to the ground. But this is never done in the streets, where they merely make a motion as if they were going to kneel. When they salute a person of rank, they bend the knee in such a manner as to touch the ground with their fingers.

We are shown the same thing equally well, or better, in China; where, among the specified gradations of obeisance, the third is defined as bending the knee, and the fourth as actual kneeling. Manifestly that which still survives among ourselves as the curtesy with the one sex, and that which until recently survived with the other sex as the scrape (made by a backward sweep of the right foot), are both of them vanishing forms of the going down on one knee.

There remains only the accompanying bend of the body. This, while the first motion passed through in making a complete prostration, is also the last motion that survives as the prostration becomes stage by stage abridged. In various places we meet indications of this transition. 'Among the Soosoos, even the wives of a great man, when speaking to him, bend their bodies, and place one hand upon each knee; this is done also when passing by.' In Samoa, 'in passing through a room where a chief is sitting, it is disrespectful to walk erect; the person must pass along with his body bent downwards'. Of the ancient Mexicans who, during an assembly, crouched before their chief, we read that 'when they retired, it was done with the head lowered'. And then in the Chinese ritual of ceremony, obeisance number two, less humble than bending the knee, is bowing low with the hands joined. Bearing in mind that there are insensible transitions between the humble salaam of the Hindoo, the profound bow which in Europe shows great respect, and the moderate bend of the head expressive of consideration, we cannot doubt that the familiar and sometimes scarcely-perceptible nod, is the last trace of the prostration.

These several abridgments of the prostration which we see occur in doing political homage and social homage, occur also in doing religious homage. Of the Congoese, Bastian says that when they have to speak to a superior —

> They kneel, turn the face half aside, and stretch out the hands towards the person addressed, which they strike together at every address. They might have sat as models to the Egyptian priests when making the representations on the temple walls, so striking is the resemblance between what is represented there and what actually takes place here.

And we may note kindred parallelisms in European religious observances. There is the going on both knees and the going on one knee; and there are the bowings and curtseyings on certain occasions at the name of Christ.

As already explained, along with the act expressing humility, the complete obeisance includes some act expressing gratification. To propitiate the superior effectually it is needful at once to imply — 'I am your slave', and — 'I love you'.

Certain of the instances cited above have exemplified the union of these two factors. Along with the attitude of abject submission assumed by the Batoka, we saw that there go rhythmic blows of the hands against the thighs. In some of the cases named, clapping of the hands, also indicating joy, was described as being an accompaniment of movements showing subjection; and many others may be added. Nobles who approach the king of Loango, 'clap their hands two or three times, and then cast themselves at his majesty's feet into the sand'. Speke says of certain attendants of the king of Uganda, that they 'threw themselves in line upon their bellies, and, wriggling like fish whilst they continued floundering, kicking about their legs, rubbing their faces, and patting their hands upon the ground'. Going on their knees to superiors, the Balonda 'continue the salutation of clapping the hands until the great ones have passed'; and a like use of the hands occurs in Dahomey. A further rhythmical movement having like meaning must be added. Already we have seen that jumping, as a natural sign of delight, is a friendly salute among the Fuegians, and that it recurs in Loango as a mark of respect to the king. Africa furnishes another instance. Grant narrates that the king of Karague 'received the salutations of his people, who, one by one, shrieked and sprang in front of him, swearing allegiance'. Let such saltatory movements be systematized, as they are likely to be during social progress, and they will constitute the dancing with which a ruler is sometimes saluted; as in the before-named case of the king of Bogotá, and as in the case Williams gives in his account of Fiji, where an inferior chief and his suite, entering the royal presence, 'performed a dance, which they finished by presenting their clubs and upper dresses to the Somo-Somo king'.

Of the other simulated signs of pleasure commonly forming part of the obeisance, kissing is the most conspicuous. This, of course, has to take such form as consists with the humility of the prostration or kindred attitude. As shown in certain foregoing instances, we have kissing the earth when the superior cannot be approached close enough for kissing the feet or the garment. Others may be added. 'It is the custom at Eboe, when the king is out, and indeed indoors as well, for the principal people to kneel on the ground and kiss it three times when he passes'; and the ancient Mexican ambassadors, on coming to Cortes, 'first touched the ground with their hands and then kissed it'. This, in the ancient East, expressed submission of conquered to conqueror; and is said to have gone as far as kissing the footmarks of a conqueror's horse. Abyssinia, where the despotism is extreme and the obeisances servile, supplies a modification. In Shoa, kissing the nearest inanimate object belonging to a superior or a benefactor, is a sign of respect and thanks. From this we pass to licking the feet and kissing the feet. Of a Malagasy chief Drury says – 'he had scarcely seated himself at his door, when his wife came out crawling on her hands and knees till she came to him, and then licked his feet . . . all the women in the town saluted their husbands in the same manner'. Slaves did the like to their masters. So in ancient Peru, 'when the chiefs came before [Atahuallpa], they made great obeisances, kissing his feet and hands'. Egyptian wall-paintings represent this extreme homage; and in Assyrian records Sennacherib mentions that Menahem of Smaria came up to bring presents and to kiss his feet. 'Kissing his feet' was part of the reverence shown to Christ by the woman with the box of ointment. At the present day among the Arabs, inferiors kiss the feet, the knees, or the garments of their superiors. Kissing the Sultan's feet is a usage in Turkey; and Sir R.K. Porter narrates that in acknowledgment of a present, a Persian 'threw himself on the ground, kissed my knees and my feet'.

Kissing the hand is a less humiliating observance than kissing the feet; mainly, perhaps, because it does not involve a prostration. This difference of implication is recognized in regions remote from one another. In Tonga, 'when a person salutes a superior relation, he kisses the hand of the party; if a very superior relation, he kisses the foot'. And the women who wait on the Arabian princesses, kiss their hands when they do them the favour not to suffer them to kiss their feet or the borders of their robes. The prevalence of this obeisance as expressing loving submission, is so great as to render illustration superfluous.

What is implied, where, instead of kissing another's hand, the person making the obeisance kisses his own hand? Does the one symbolize the other, as being the nearest approach to it possible under the circumstances This appears a hazardous inference; but there is evidence justifying it. D'Arvieux says —

> An oriental pays his respects to a person of superior station by kissing his hand and putting it to his forehead; but if the superior be of a condescending temper, he will snatch away his hand as soon as the other has touched it; then the inferior puts his own fingers to his lips and afterwards to his forehead.

This, I think, makes it clear that the common custom of kissing the hand to another, originally expressed the wish, or the willingness, to kiss his hand.

Here, as before, the observance, beginning as a spontaneous propitiation of conqueror by conquered, of master by slave, of ruler by ruled, early passes into a religious propitiation also. To the ghost, and to the deity developed from the ghost, these actions of love and liking are used. That embracing and kissing of the lower extremities, which was among the Hebrews an obeisance to the living person, Egyptian wall-paintings represent as an obeisance made to the mummy enclosed in its case; and then, in pursuance of this action, we have kissing the feet of statues of gods in pagan Rome and of holy images among Christians. Ancient Mexico furnished an instance of the transition from kissing the ground as a political obeisance, to a modified kissing the ground as a religious obeisance. Describing an oath Clavigero says — 'Then naming the principal god, or any other they particularly reverenced, they kissed their hand, after having touched the earth with it.' In Peru 'the manner of worship was to open the hands, to make some noise with the lips as of kissing, and to ask what they wished, at the same time offering the sacrifice', and Garcilasso, describing the libation to the Sun, adds — 'At the same time they kissed the air two or three times, which was a token of adoration among these Indians.' Nor have European races failed to furnish kindred facts. Kissing the hand to the statue of a god was a Roman form of adoration.

Once more, saltatory movements, which being natural expressions of delight become complimentary acts before a visible ruler, become acts of worship before an invisible ruler. David danced before the ark. Dancing was originally a religious ceremony among the Greeks; from the earliest times the 'worship of Apollo was connected with a religious dance'. King Pepin, 'like King David, forgetful of the regal purple, in his joy bedowed his costly robes with tears and danced before the relics of the blessed martyr'. And in the Middle Ages there were religious dances in churches; as there are still in Christian churches at Jerusalem.

To interpret another series of observances we must go back to the prostration in its original form. I refer to those expressions of submission which are made by putting dust or ashes on some part of the body.

Men cannot roll over in the sand in front of their king or crawl before him, or repeatedly knock their heads against the ground, without soiling themselves. Hence the adhering dirt is recognized as a concomitant mark of subjection; and comes to be gratuitously assumed, and artificially increased, in the anxiety to propitiate. Already the association between this act and the act of prostration has been incidentally exemplified by cases from Africa; and Africa furnishes other cases which exemplify more fully this self-defiling as a distinct form. 'In the Congo regions prostration is made, the earth is kissed, and dust is strewed over the forehead and arms, before every Banza or village chief', and Burton adds that the Dahoman salutation consists of two actions – prostration and pouring sand or earth upon the head. Similarly 'in saluting a stranger, they [the Kakanda people on the Niger] stoop almost to the earth, throwing dust on their foreheads several times.' And among the Balonda,

> The inferiors, on meeting their superiors in the street, at once drop on their knees and rub dust on their arms and chest. During an oration to a person commanding respect, the speaker every two or three seconds 'picked up a little sand, and rubbed it on the upper part of his arms and chest'. When they wish to be excessively polite, they bring a quantity of ashes or pipeclay in a piece of skin, and, taking up handfuls, rub it on the chest and upper front part of each arm.

Moreover, we are shown how in this case, as in all other cases, the ceremony undergoes abridgment. Of these same Balonda, Livingstone says, 'the chiefs go through the manœuvre of rubbing the sand on the arms, but only make a feint of picking up some'. On the Lower Niger, the people when making prostrations 'cover them [their heads] repeatedly with sand; or at all events they go through the motion of doing so. Women, on perceiving their friends, kneel immediately, and pretend to pour sand alternately over each arm'. In Asia this ceremony was, and still is, performed with like meaning. As expressing political humiliation it was adopted by the priests who, when going to implore Florus to spare the Jews, appeared 'with dust sprinkled in great plenty upon their heads, with bosoms deprived of any covering but what was rent'. In Turkey, abridgments of the obeisance may yet be witnessed. At a review, even officers on horseback, saluting their superiors, 'go through the form of throwing dust over their heads'; and when a caravan of pilgrims started, spectators 'went through the pantomime of throwing dirt over their heads'.

Hebrew records prove that this sign of submission made before visible persons, was made before invisible persons also. Along with those blood-lettings and markings of the flesh and cuttings of the hair which, at funerals, were used to propitiate the ghost, there went the putting of ashes on the head. The like was done to propitiate the deity; as when 'Joshua rent his clothes, and fell to the earth upon his face before the ark of the Lord until the eventide, he and the elders of Israel, and put dust upon their heads'. Even still this usage occurs among Catholics on occasions of special humiliation.

We must again return to that original obeisance which first actually is, and then which simulates, the attitude of the conquered before the conqueror, to find the clue to certain further movements signifying submission. As described in a foregoing paragraph, the supplicating Khond 'throws himself on his face with hands joined'. Whence this attitude of the hands?

From the usages of a people among whom submission and all marks of it were carried to great extremes, an instance has already been given indicating the genesis of this action. A sign of humility in ancient Peru was to have the hands bound and a rope round the neck: the condition of captives was simulated. Did there need proof that it has been a common practice to make prisoners of war defenceless by tying their hands, I might begin with Assyrian wall-sculptures, in which men thus bound are represented; but the fact that among ourselves, men charged with crimes are hand-cuffed by the police when taken, shows how naturally suggested is this method of rendering prisoners impotent. And for concluding that bound hands hence came to be an adopted mark of subjection, further reason is furnished by two strange customs found in Africa and Asia respectively. When the king of Uganda returned the visit of captains Speke and Grant, 'his brothers, a mob of little ragamuffins, several in handcuffs, sat behind him. It was said that the king, before coming to the throne, always went about in irons, as his small brothers now do.' And then, among the Chinese, 'on the third day after the birth of a child the ceremony of binding its wrists is observed. These things are worn till the child is fourteen days old sometimes for several months, or even for a year. It is thought that such a tying of the wrists will tend to keep the child from being troublesome in after life.'

Such indications of its origin, joined with such examples of derived practices, force on us the inference that raising the joined hands as part of that primitive obeisance signifying absolute submission, was an offering of the hands to be bound. The above-described attitude of the Khond exhibits the proceeding in its original form; and on reading in Hue that 'the Mongul hunter saluted us, with his clasped hands raised to his forehead', or in Drury that when the Malagasy approach a great man, they hold the hands up in a supplicatory form, we cannot doubt that this act now expresses reverence because it originally implied subjugation. Of the Siamese, La Loubere says — 'If you extend your hand to a Siamese, to place it in his, he carried both his hands to yours, as if to place himself entirely in your power.' That presentation of the joined hands has the meaning here suggested, is elsewhere shown. In Unyanyembe, 'when two of them meet, the Wezee puts both his palms together, these are gently clasped by the Watusi' [a man of more powerful race]; and in Sumatra, the obeisance 'consists in being the body, and the inferior's putting his joined hands between those of the superior, and then lifting them to his forehead'. By these instances we are reminded that a kindred act was once a form of submission in Europe. When doing homage, the vassal, on his knees, placed his joined hands between the hands of his suzerain.

As in foregoing cases, an attitude signifying defeat and therefore political subordination, becomes an attitude of religious devotion. By the Mahommedan worshipper we are shown that same clasping of the hands above the head which expresses reverence for a living superior. Among the Greeks, 'the Olympian gods were prayed to in an upright position with raised hands; the marine gods with hands held horizontally; the gods of Tartarus with hands held down'. And the presentation of the hands joined palm to palm, once throughout Europe required from an inferior when professing obedience to a superior, is still taught to children as the attitude of prayer.

A kindred use of the hands descends into social intercourse; and in the far East the filiation continues to be clear. 'When the Siamese salute one another, they join the hands, raising them before the face or above the head.' Of the eight obeisances in China, the least profound is that of putting the hands together and raising them before the breast. Even among ourselves a remnant of this action is traceable. An obsequious shopman or fussy innkeeper, may be seen to join and loosely move the slightly raised hands one over another, in a way suggestive of derivation from this primitive sign of submission.

A group of obeisances having a connected, though divergent, root, come next to be dealt with. Those which we have thus far considered do not directly affect the subject person's dress. But from modifications of dress, either in position, state, or kind, a series of ceremonial observances result.

The conquered man, prostrate before his conqueror, and becoming himself a possession, simultaneously loses possession of whatever things he has about him; and therefore, surrendering his weapons, he also yields up, if the victor demands it, whatever part of his dress is worth taking. Hence the nakedness, partial or complete, of the captive, becomes additional evidence of his subjugation. That it was so regarded of old in the East, there is clear proof. In Isaiah 20:2-4, we read — 'And the Lord said, like as my servant Isaiah hath walked naked and barefoot three years for a sign so shall the king of Assyria lead away the Egyptians prisoners, and the Ethiopians captives, young and old, naked and barefoot.' And that the Assyrians completely stripped their captives is shown by their sculptures. Nay, even our own days furnish evidence; as at the beginning of the Afghan war, when the Afreedees were reported to have stripped certain prisoners they had taken. Naturally, then, the taking off and yielding up of clothing becomes a mark of political submission, and in some cases even a complimentary observance. In Fiji, on the day for paying tribute —

> The chief of Somo-Somo, who had previously stripped off his robes, then sat down, and removed even the train or covering, which was of immense length, from his waist. He gave it to the speaker, who gave him in return a piece large enough only for the purposes of decency. The rest of the Somo-Somo chiefs, each of whom on coming on the ground had a train of several yards in length, stripped themselv entirely, left their trains, and walked away thus leaving all the Somo-Somo people naked.

Further we read that during Cook's stay at Tahiti, two men of superior rank 'came on board, and each singled out his friend . . . this ceremony consisted in taking off great part of their clothes and putting them upon us'. And then in another Polynesian island, Samoa, this complimentary act is greatly abridged: only the girdle is presented.

With such facts to give us the clue, we can scarcely doubt that surrender of clothing originates those obeisances which are made by uncovering the body, more or less extensively. All degrees of uncovering having this meaning. From Ibu Batuta's account of his journey into the Soudan, Mr Tylor cites the statement that 'women may only come unclothed into the presence of the Sultan of Melli, and even the Sultan's own daughters must conform to the custom'; and what doubt we might reasonably feel as to the existence of an obeisance thus carried to its original extreme, is removed on reading in Speke that at the present time, at the court of Uganda, 'stark-naked, full-grown women are the valets'. Elsewhere in Africa an incomplete, though still considerable, unclothing as an obeisance occurs. In Abyssinia inferiors bare their bodies down to the girdle in presence of superiors; 'but to equals the corner of the cloth is removed only for a time.' The like occurs in Polynesia. The Tahitians uncover 'the body as low as the waist, in the presence of the king'; and in the Society Isles generally, 'the lower ranks of people, by way of respect, strip off their upper garment in the presence of their' principal chiefs. How this obeisance becomes further abridged, and how it becomes extended to other persons than rulers, is shown by natives of the Gold Coast.

> They also salute Europeans, and sometimes each other, by slightly removing their robe from their left shoulder with the right hand, gracefully bowing at the same time. When they wish to be very respectful, they uncover the shoulder altogether, and support the robe under the arm, the whole of the person from the breast upwards being left exposed.

And Burton says that, 'throughout Yoruba and the Gold Coast, to bare the shoulders is like unhatting in England'.

Evidently uncovering the head, thus suggestively compared with uncovering the upper part of the body, has the same original meaning. Even in certain European usages the relation between the two has been recognized; as by Ford, who remarks that 'uncloaking in Spain is equivalent to our taking off the hat'. It is recognized in Africa itself where, as in Dahomey, the two are joined: 'the men bared their shoulders, doffing their caps and large umbrella hats', says Burton, speaking of his reception. It is recognized in Polynesia, where, as in Tahiti, along with the stripping down to the waist before the king, there goes uncovering of the head. Hence it seems that removal of the hat among European peoples, often reduced among ourselves to touching the hat, is a remnant of that process of unclothing himself, by which, in early times, the captive expressed the yielding up of all he had.

That baring the feet has the same origin, is well shown by these same Gold Coast natives; for while they partially bare the upper part of the body, they also take off their sandals 'as a mark of respect': they begin to strip the body at both ends. Throughout ancient America uncovering the feet had a like meaning. In Peru, 'no lord, however great he might be, entered the presence of the Ynca in rich clothing, but in humble attire and barefooted'; and in Mexico, 'the kings who were vassals of Montezuma were obliged to take off their shoes when they came into his presence': the significance of this act being so great that as 'Michoaca was independent of Mexico, the sovereign took the title of cazonzi – tha is, "shod". Kindred accounts of Asiatics have made the usage familiar to us. In Burmah, 'even in the streets and highways, a European, if he meets with the king, or joins his party, is obliged to take off his shoes'. And in Persia, every one who approaches the royal presence must bare his feet.

Verification of these interpretations is yielded by the equally obvious interpretations of certain usages which we similarly meet with in societies where extreme expressions of subjection are required. I refer to the appearing in presence of rulers dressed in coarse clothing – the clothing of slaves. In Mexico, whenever Montezuma's attendants 'entered his apartments, they had first to take off their rich costumes and put on meaner garments'. In Peru, along with the rule that a subject should appear before the Inca with a burden on his back, simulating servitude, and along with the rule that he should be barefooted, further simulating servitude, there went, as we have seen, the rule that 'no lord, however great he might be, entered the presence of the Inca in rich clothing, but in humble attire', again simulating servitude. A kindred though less extreme usage exists in Dahomey: the highest subjects may 'ride on horseback, be carried in hammocks, wear silk, maintain a numerous retinue, with large umbrellas of their own order, flags, trumpets, and other musical instruments; but, on their entrance at the royal gate, all these insignia are laid aside'. Even in mediæval Europe, submission was expressed by taking off those parts of the dress and appendages which were inconsistent with the appearance of servitude. Thus, in France, in 1467, the head men of a town, surrendering to a victorious duke, 'brought to his camp with them three hundred of the best citizens in their shirts, bareheaded, and barelegged, who presented the keies of the citie to him, and yielded themselves to his mercy'. And the doing of feudal homage included observances of kindred meaning Saint Simon, describing one of the latest instances, and naming among ceremonies gone through the giving up of belt, sword, gloves, and hat, says that this was done 'to strip the vassal of his marks of dignity in the presence of his lord'. So that whether it be the putting on of coarse clothing or the putting off of fine clothing, the meaning is the same.

... Nor must we omit to note that obeisances of this class, too, made first to supreme persons and presently to less powerful persons, diffuse gradually until they become general. Quotations above given have shown incidentally that in Africa partial uncovering of the shoulder is a salute between equals, and that a kindred removal of the cloak in Spain serves a like purpose. Similarly, the going barefoot into a king's presence, and into a temple, originates an ordinary civility. The Damaras take off their sandals before entering a stranger's house; a Japanese leaves his shoes at the door, even when he enters a shop; 'upon entering a Turkish house, it is the invariable rule to leave the outer slipper or galosh at the foot of the stairs'. And then in Europe, from having been a ceremony of feudal homage and of religious worship, uncovering the head has become an expression of respect due even to a labourer on entering his cottage. ...

FORMS OF ADDRESS

Along with other ways of propitiating the victor, the master, the ruler, will naturally come speeches which, beginning with confessions of defeat by verbal assumptions of its attitude, will develop into varied phrases acknowledging servitude. The implication, therefore, is that forms of address in general, descending as they do from these originals, will express, clearly or vaguely, ownership by, or subjection to, the person addressed.

Of propitiatory speeches there are some which, instead of describing the prostration entailed by defeat, describe the resulting state of being at the mercy of the person addressed. One of the strangest of these occurs among the cannibal Tupis. While, on the one hand, a warrior shouts to his enemy – 'May every misfortune come upon thee, my meat!' on the other hand, the speech required from the captive Hans Stade on approaching a dwelling, was – 'I, your food, have come': that is – my life is at your disposal. Then, again, instead of professing to live only by permission of the superior, actual or pretended, who is spoken to, we find the speaker professing to be personally a chattel of his, or to be holding property at his disposal, or both. Africa, Asia, Polynesia, and Europe, furnish examples. 'When a stranger enters the house of a Serracolet (Inland Negro), he goes out and says – "White man, my house, my wife, my children belong to thee" '. Around Delhi, if you ask an inferior "Whose horse is that?" he says "Slave's', meaning his own; or he may say – "It is your highnesses', meaning that, being his, it is at your disposal". In the Sandwich Islands a chief, asked respecting the ownership of a house or canoe possessed by him, replies – 'It is yours and mine'. In France, in the fifteenth century, a complimentary speech made by an abbé on his knees to the queen when visiting a monastery was – 'We resign and offer up the abbey with all that is in it, our bodies, as our goods.' And at the present time in Spain, where politeness requires that anything admired by a visitor shall be offered to him, 'the correct place of dating [a letter] from should be from this *your* house, wherever it is; you must not say from this *my* house, as you mean to place it at the disposition of your correspondent'.

But these modes of addressing a real or fictitious superior, indirectly asserting subjection to him in body and effects, are secondary in importance to the direct assertions of slavery and servitude; which, beginning in barbarous days, have persisted down to the present time.

Hebrew narratives have familiarized us with the word 'servant', as applied to himself by a subject or inferior, when speaking to a ruler or superior. In our days of freedom, the associations established by daily habit have obscured the fact that 'servant' as used in translations of old records, means 'slave' – implies the condition fallen into by a captive taken in war. Consequently when, as often in the Bible, the phrases 'thy servant' or 'thy servants' are uttered before a king, they must be taken to signify that same state of subjugation which is more circuitously signified by the phrases quoted in the last section. Clearly this self-abasing word was employed, not by attendants only, but by conquered peoples, and by subjects at large; as we see when the unknown David, addressing Saul, describes both himself and his father as Saul's servants. And kindred uses of the word to rulers have continued down to modern times.

Very early, however, professions of servitude, orginally made only to one of supreme authority, came to be made to those of subordinate authority. Brought before Joseph in Egypt, and fearing him, his brethren call themselves his servants or slaves; and not only so, but speak of their father as standing in a like relation to him. Moreover, there is evidence that this form of address extended to the intercourse between equals where a favour was to be gained; as witness Judges 19:19. And we have seen in the last section that even still in India, a man shows his politeness by calling himself the slave of the person addressed. How in Europe a like diffusion has taken place, need not be shown further than by exemplifying some of the stages. Among French courtiers in the sixteenth century it was common to say – 'I am your servant and the perpetual slave of your house'; and among ourselves in past times there were used such indirect expressions of servitude as – 'Yours to command', 'Ever at your worship's disposing'.'In all serviceable humbleness', &c. While in our days, rarely made orally save in irony, such forms have left only their written representatives – 'Your obedient servant', 'Your humble servant'; reserved for occasions when distance is to be maintained, and for this reason often having inverted meanings.

That for religious purposes the same propitiatory words are employed, is a familiar truth. In Hebrew history men are described as servants of God, just as they are described as servants of the king. Neighbouring peoples are said to serve their respective deities just as slaves are said to serve their masters. And there are cases in which these relations to the visible ruler and to the invisible ruler, are expressed in like ways; as where we read that 'The king hath fulfilled the request of his servant', and elsewhere that 'The Lord hath redeemed his servant Jacob'. Hence as used in worship, the expression 'thy servant' has originated as have all other elements of religious ceremonial.

And here better than elsewhere, may be noted the fact that the phrase 'thy son', used to a ruler or superior, or other person, is originally equivalent to 'thy servant'. On remembering that in rude societies children exist only on sufferance of their parents; and that in patriarchal groups the father had life and death power over his children; we see that professing to be another's son was like professing to be his servant or slave. There are ancient examples demonstrating the equivalence; as when 'Ahaz sent messengers to Tiglath-pileser king of Assyria, saying, I am thy servant and thy son: come up and save me'. Mediæval Europe furnished instances when, as we saw, rulers offered themselves for adoption by more powerful rulers: so assuming the condition of filial servitude and calling themselves sons; as did Theodebert I and Childebert II to the emperors Justinian and Maurice. Nor does there lack evidence that this expression of subordination spreads like the rest, until it becomes a complimentary form of speech. At the present time in India, the man who in compliment professes to be your slave, will, on introducing his son say – 'This is your highness's son'. And 'a Samoan cannot use more persuasive language than to call himself the son of the person addressed'.

From those complimentary phrases which express abasement of self, we pass to those which exalt another. Either kind taken alone, is a confession of relative inferiority; and this confession gains in emphasis when the two kinds are joined, as they commonly are.

At first it does not seem likely that eulogies may, like other propitiations, be traced back to the behaviour of the conquered to the conqueror; but we have proof that they do thus originate, certainly in some cases. To the victorious Ramses II his defeated foes preface their prayers for mercy by the laudatory words – 'Prince guarding thy army, valiant with the sword, bulwark of his troops in day of battle, king mighty of strength, great Sovran, Sun powerful in truth, approved of Ra, mighty in victories, Ramses Miamon'. Obviously there is no separation between such praises uttered by the vanquished, and those afterwards coming from them as a subject people. We pass without break to glorifying words like those addressed to the king of Siam – 'Mighty and august lord! Divine Mercy!' 'The Divine Order!' 'The Master of Life!' 'Sovereign of the Earth!' or those addressed to the Sultan – 'The Shadow of God!' 'Glory of the Universe!' or those addressed to the Chinese Emperor – 'Son of Heaven!' 'The Lord of Ten Thousand Years!' or those some years since addressed by the Bulgarians to the emperor of

Russia – 'O blessed Czar!' 'Blissful Czar!' 'Orthodox powerful Czar!' or those with which, in the past, speeches to the French monarch commenced – 'O very benign! O very great! O very merciful!' And then along with these propitiations by direct flattery, there go others in which the flattery is indirectly conveyed by affected admiration of whatever the ruler says; as when the courtiers of the kind of Delhi held up their hands crying – 'Wonder, wonder!' after any ordinary speech; or in broad day, if he said it was night, responded – 'Behold the moon and the stars!' or as when Russians in past times exclaimed – 'God and the prince have willed!' God and the prince know!'

Eulogistic phrases first used to supreme men, descend to men of less authority, and so downwards. Examples may be taken from those current in France during the sixteenth century – to a cardinal, 'the very illustrious and very reverend'; to a marquis, 'my very illustrious and much-honoured lord'; to a doctor, 'the virtuous and excellent'. And from our own past days may be added such complimentary forms of address as – 'the right worshipful', to knights and sometimes to esquires; 'the right noble', 'the honourable-minded', used to gentlemen; and even to men addressed as Mr., such laudatory prefixes as 'the worthy and worshipful'. Along with flattering epithets there spread more involved flatteries, especially observable in the East, where both are extreme. On a Chinese invitation-card the usual compliment is – 'To what an elevation of splendour will your presence assist us to rise!' Tavernier, from whom I have quoted the above example of scarcely credible flattery from the Court of Delhi, adds, 'this vice passeth even unto the people', and he says that his military attendant, compared to the greatest of conquerors, was described as making the world tremble when he mounted his horse. In these parts of India at the present day, an ordinary official is addressed – 'My lord, there are only two who can do anything for me: God is the first, and you are second'; or sometimes, as a correspondent writes to me – ' "Above is God, and your honour is below"; "Your honour has power to do anything"; "You are our king and lord"; "You are in God's place" '.

On reading that in Tavernier's time a usual expression in Persia was – 'Let the king's will be done', recalling the parallel expression – 'Let God's will be done', we are reminded that various of the glorifying speeches made to kings parallel those made to deities. Where the militant type is highly developed, and where divinity is ascribed to the monarch, not only after death but before, as of old in Egypt and Peru, and as now in Japan, China, and Siam, it naturally results that the eulogies of visible rulers and of rulers who have become invisible, are the same. Having reached the extreme of hyperbole to the king when living, they cannot go further to the king when dead and deified. And the identity thus initiated continues through subsequent stages with deities whose origins are no longer traceable.

Into the complete obeisance we saw that there enter two elements, one implying submission and the other implying love; and into the complete form of address two analogous elements enter. With words employed to propitiate by abasing self or elevating the person addressed, or both, are joined words suggestive of attachment to him — wishes for his life, health, and happiness. . . .

Since they state in words what obeisances express by acts, forms of address of course have the same general relations to social types. The parallelisms must be noted.

Speaking of the Dacotahs, who are politically unorganized, and who had not even nominal chiefs till the whites began to make distinctions among them, Burton says — 'Ceremony and manners in our sense of the word they have none'; and he instances the entrance of a Dacotah into a stranger's house with a mere exclamation meaning 'well'. Bailey remarks of the Veddahs that in addressing others, 'they use none of the honorifics so profusely common in singhalese; the pronoun "*lo*" "thou", being alone used, whether they are addressing each other or those whose position would entitle them to outward respect." These cases will sufficiently indicate the general fact that where there is no subordination, speeches which elevate the person spoken to and abase the person speaking, do not arise. Conversely, where personal government is absolute, verbal self-humiliations and verbal exaltations of others assume exaggerated forms. Among the Siamese, who are all slaves of the king, an inferior calls himself dust under the feet of a superior, while ascribing to the superior transcendent powers; and the forms of address, even between equals, avoid naming the person addressed. In China, where there is no check on the power of the 'Imperial Supreme', the phrases of adulation and humility, first used in intercourse with rulers and afterwards spreading, have elaborated to such extremes that in inquiring another's name the form is — 'May I presume to ask what is your noble surname and your eminent name'; while the reply is —'The name of my cold (or poor) family is —, and my ignoble name is —.' If we ask where ceremony has initiated the most elaborate misuses of pronouns, we find them in Japan, where wars long ago established a despotism which acquired divine prestige.

Similarly, on contrasting the Europe of past times, characterized by social structures developed by, and fitted for, perpetual fighting, with modern Europe, in which, though fighting on a large scale occurs, it is the temporary rather than the permanent form of social activity, we observe that complimentary expressions, now less used, are also now less exaggerated. Nor does the generalization fail when we compare the modern European societies that are organized in high degrees for war, like those of the Continent, with our own society, not so well organized for war; or when we compare the regulative parts of our own society, which are developed by militancy, with the industrial parts. Flattering superlatives and expressions of devotion are less profuse here than abroad; and much as the use of complimentary language has diminished among our ruling classes in recent times, there remains a greater use of it among them than among the industrial classes: especially those of the industrial classes who have no direct relations with the ruling classes.

Though the more general names father, king, elder, and their derivatives, which afterwards arise, are not directly militant in their implications, yet they are indirectly so; for they are the names of rulers evolved by militant activity, who habitually exercise militant functions: being in early stages always the commanders of their subjects in battle. Down to our most familiar titles we have this genesis implied. 'Esquire' and 'Mister' are derived the one from the name of a knight's attendant and the other from the name *magister* — originally a ruler or chief, who was a military head by origin and a civil head by development.

As in other cases, comparisons of societies of different types disclose this relation in another way. Remarking that in sanguinary and despotic Dahomey, the personal name 'can hardly be said to exist; it changes with every rank of the holder', Burton says — 'The dignities seem to be interminable; except amongst the slaves and the *canaille*, "handles" are the rule, not the exception, and most of them are hereditary.' So, too, under Oriental despotisms. 'The name of every Burman disappears when he gets a title of rank or office, and is heard no more'; and in China, 'there are twelve orders of nobility, conferred solely on the members of the imperial house or clan', besides 'the five ancient orders of nobility'. Europe supplies further evidence. Travellers in both Russia and Germany, with their social organizations adapted to war, comment on the 'insane rage for titles of every description': the results being that in Russia 'a police-office clerk belongs to the eighteenth grade, and has the right to the title of Your Honour'; and in Germany the names of rank and names of office so abundantly distributed, are habitually expected and studiously given, in both speech and writing. Meanwhile England, for ages past less militant in type, has ever shown this trait in a smaller degree; and along with the growth of industrialism and accompanying changes of organization, the use of titles in social intercourse has decreased.

With equal clearness is this connexion seen within each society. By the thirteen grades in our army and the fourteen grades in our navy, we are shown that the exclusively-militant structures continue to be characterized in the highest degree by numerous and specific titular marks. To the ruling classes, descendants or representatives of those who in past times were heads of military forces, the higher distinctions of rank still mostly belong; and of remaining titles, the ecclesiastical and legal are also associated with the regulative organization developed by militancy. Meanwhile, the producing and exchanging parts of the society, carrying on industrial activities, only in exceptional cases bear any titles beyond those which, descending and spreading, have almost lost their meanings.

It is indisputable, then, that serving first to commemorate the triumphs of savages over their foes, titles have expanded, multiplied, and differentiated, as conquests have formed large societies by consolidation and re-consolidation of small ones; and that, belonging to the social type generated by habitual war, they tend to lose their uses and their values, in proportion as this type is replaced by one fitted for carrying on the pursuits of peace.

The idea of relative height and the idea of relative wealth, appear to join in originating certain building regulations expressive of class-distinctions. An elevated abode implies at once display of riches and assumption of a position overlooking others. Hence, in various places, limitations of the heights to which different ranks may build. In ancient Mexico, under Montezuma's laws, 'no one was allowed to build a house with [several] stories, except the great lords and gallant captains, on pain of death'. A kindred regulation exists at the present time in Dahomey; where the king, wishing to honour some one, 'gave him a formal leave to build a house two stories high'; and where 'the palace and the city gates are allowed five surish [steps]; chiefs have four tall or five short, and all others three, or as the king directs'. There are restrictions of like kind in Japan. 'The height of the street-front, and even the number of windows, are determined by sumptuary laws.' So, too, is it in Burmah. Yule says: 'The character of house, and especially of roof, appropriate to each rank, appears to be matter of regulation, or inviolable prescription'; and, according to Sangermano, 'nothing less than death can expiate the crime, either of choosing a shape [for a house] that does not belong to the dignity of the master, or of painting the house white; which colour is permitted to the members of the royal family alone'. More detailed are the interdicts named by Syme.

Piasath, the regal spire, distinguishes the dwellings of the monarch and the temples of the divinity. To none other is it allowed. . . . There are no brick buildings either in Pegue or Rangoon except such as belong to the king, or are dedicated to their divinity Gaudama. Gilding is forbidden to all subjects of the Birman Empire. Liberty even to lacker and paint the pillars of their houses, is granted to very few.

Along with laws forbidding those of inferior rank to have the higher and more ornamental houses which naturally imply the wealth that accompanies power, there go interdicts on the use by common people of various appliances to comfort which the man of rank and influence has. Among these may first be noted artificial facilities for locomotion.

A sketch in an African book of travels, representing the king of Obbo making a progress, seated on the shoulders of an attendant, shows us in its primitive form, the connexion between being carried by other men and the exercise of power over other men. Marking, by implication, a ruling person, the palanquin or equivalent vehicle is in many places forbidden to inferior persons. Among the ancient Chibehas, 'the law did not allow any one to be carried in a litter on the shoulders of his men, except the Bagota and those to whom he gave the privilege'. Prior to the year 1821, no person in Madagascar 'was allowed to ride in the native chair or palanquin, except the royal family, the judges, and first officers of state'. So, too, in Europe, there have been restrictions on the use of such chairs. Among the Romans, 'in town only the senators and ladies were allowed to be carried in them'; and in France, in past times, the sedan was forbidden to those below a certain rank. In some places the social *status* of the occupant is indicated by the more or less costly accompaniments. Kœmpfer says that in Japan, 'the bigness and length of these [sedan] poles hath been determined by the political laws of the empire, proportionable to every one's quality'. The sedan 'is carried by two, four, eight or more men, according to the quality of the person in it'. The like happens in China. 'The highest officers are carried by eight bearers, others by four, and the lowest by two: this, and every other particular, being regulated by laws.' Then, elsewhere, the character of appliances for locomotion on water is similarly prescribed. In Turkey, 'the hierarchy of rank is maintained and designated by the size of each Turkish functionary's boat'; and in Siam 'the height and ornaments of the cabin [in barges] designate the rank or the functions of the occupier'.

As the possession of chair-bearers, who in early stages are slaves, implies alike the mastery and the wealth always indicative of rank in societies of militant type; so, too, does possession of attendants to carry umbrellas or other protections against the sun. Hence interdicts on the use of these by inferiors. Such restrictions occur in comparatively early stages. In Fiji (Somo-somo) only the king and the two high priests in favour, can use the sun-shade. In Congo only those of royal blood are allowed to use an umbrella, or to be carried in a mat. The sculptured records of extinct eastern peoples, imply the existence of this class-mark. Among the Assyrians,

> the officers in close attendance upon the monarch varied according

to his employment. In war he was accompanied by his chariotee, his shield-bearer or shield-bearers, his groom, his quiver-bearer, his mace-bearer, and sometimes by his parasol-bearer. In peace the parasol-bearer is always represented as in attendance, except in hunting expeditions, or where he is replaced by a fan-bearer.

Adjacent parts of the world show use the same mark of distinction in use down to the present time. 'From India to Abyssinia', says Burton, 'the umbrella is the sign of royalty'. Still further east this symbol of dignity is multiplied to produce the idea of greater dignity. In Siam, at the king's coronation, 'a page comes forward and presents to the king the seven-storied umbrella, – the *savetraxat* or primary symbol of royalty'. And when the emperor of China leaves his palace, he is accompanied by twenty men bearing large umbrellas and twenty fan-bearers. Elsewhere umbrellas, not monopolized by kings, may be used by others, but with differences;as in Java, where custom prescribes six colours for the umbrellas of six ranks. Evidently the shade-yielding umbrella is closely allied to the shade-yielding canopy; the use of which also is a class-distinction. Ancient America furnished a good instance. In Utlatlan the king sat under four canopies, the 'elect' under three, the chief captain under two, and the second captain under one. And here we are reminded that this developed form of the umbrella, having four supports, is alike in the East and in Europe, used in exaltation of both the divine ruler and the human ruler: in the one region borne by attendants over kings and supported in a more permanent manner over the cars in which idols are drawn; and in the other used alike in state-processions and ecclesiastical processions, to shade now the monarch and now the Host.

Of course with regulations giving to higher ranks the exclusive enjoyment of the more costly conveniences, there go others forbidding the inferior to have conveniences of even less costly natures. For example, in Fiji the best kind of mat for lying on is forbidden to the common people. In Dahomey, the use of hammocks is a royal prerogative, shared in only by the whites. Concerning the Siamese, Bowring says: 'We were informed that the use of such cushions [more or less ornamented, according to rank] was prohibited to the people'. And we learn from Bastian that among the Joloffs the use of the mosquito-curtain is a royal prerogative.

Of sumptuary laws, those regulating the uses of foods may be traced back to very early stages – stages in which usages have not yet taken the shape of laws. They go along with the subordination of the young to the old, and of females to males. Among the Tasmanians, 'the old men got the best food'; and Sturt says, 'only the old men of the natives of

Australia have the privilege of eating the emu. For a young man to eat it is a crime'. The Khond women, Macpherson tells us, 'for some unknown cause, are never, I am informed, permitted to eat the flesh of the hog'. In Tahiti 'the men were allowed to eat the flesh of the pig, and of fowls, and a variety of fish, cocoa-nuts, and plantains, and whatever was presented as an offering to the gods, which the females on pain of death, were forbidden to touch'. After stating that the Fijian women are never permitted to enter the temple, the United States' explorers add – 'nor, as we have seen, to eat human flesh, at least in public'.

Of food-restrictions other than those referring to age and sex, may first be named one from Fiji – one which also refers to the consumption of human flesh. Seeman says 'the common people throughout the group, as well as women of all classes, were by custom debarred from it. Cannibalism was thus restricted to the chiefs and gentry.' Of other class-restrictions on food, ancient America furnishes examples. Among the Chibchas, 'venison could not be eaten unless the privilege had been granted by the cazique'. In San Salvador, 'none formerly drank chocolate but the prime men and notable soldiers', and in Peru 'the kings (Yncas) had the coca as a royal possession and privilege'.

Of course there might be added to these certain of the sumptuary laws respecting food which prevailed during past times throughout Europe.

Of the various class-distinctions which imply superior rank by implying greater wealth, the most curious remain. I refer to certain inconvenient, and sometimes painful, traits, only to be acquired by those whose abundant means enable them to live without labour, or to indulge in some kind of sensual excess.

One group of these distinctions, slightly illustrated among ourselves by the pride taken in delicate hands, as indicating freedom from manual labour, is exhibited in marked forms in some societies that are comparatively little advanced. 'The chiefs in the Society Islands value themselves on having long nails on all, or on some, of their fingers.' 'Fijian kings and priests wear the finger nails long', says Jackson; and in Sumatra, 'persons of superior rank encourage the growth of their hand-nails, particularly those of the fore and little fingers, to an extraordinary length'. Everyone knows that a like usage has a like origin in China; where, however, long nails have partially lost thier meaning: upper servants being allowed to wear them. But of personal defects similarly originating, China furnishes a far more striking instance in the cramped feet of ladies. Obviously these have become signs of class-distinction, because of the implied inability to labour, and the implied possession of means sufficient to purchase attendance. Then, again, as marking rank because implying riches, we have undue, and sometimes excessive, fatness; either of the superior person himself or of his belongings. The beginnings of this may be traced in quite early stages; as among some uncivilized American peoples. 'An Indian is *respectable* in his own community, in proportion as his wife and children look fat and well fed: this being a proof of his prowess and success as a hunter, and his consequent riches.' From this case, in which the relation between implied wealth and implied power is directly recognized, we pass in the course of social development to causes in which, instead of the normal fatness indicating sufficiency, there comes the abnormal fatness indicating superfluity, and, consequently, greater wealth. In China, great fatness is a source of pride in a mandarin. Ellis tells us that corpulence is a mark of distinction among Tahitian females. Throughout Africa there prevails an admiration for corpulence in women, which, in some places, rises to a great pitch; as in Karague where the king has 'very fat wives' — where, according to Speke, the king's sister-in-law 'was another of those wonders of obesity, unable to stand excepting on all fours', and where 'as fattening is the first duty of fashionable female life, it must be duly enforced by the rod if necessary'. Still stranger are the marks of dignity constituted by diseases resulting from those excessive gratifications of appetite which wealth makes possible. Even among ourselves may be traced an association of ideas which thus originates. The story about a gentleman of the old school, who, hearing that some man of inferior extraction was suffering from gout, exclaimed — 'Damn the fellow; wasn't rheumatism good enough for him', illustrates the still-current idea that gout is a gentlemanly disease, because it results from that high living which presupposes the abundant means usually associated with superior position. Introduced by this instance, the instance which comes to us from Polynesia will seem not unnatural. 'The habitual use of ava causes a whitish scurf on the skin, which among the heathen Tahitians was reckoned a badge of nobility; the common people not having the means of indulgence requisite to produce it'.

How these further class-distinctions, though not, like preceding ones, directly traceable to militancy, are indirectly traceable to it and how they fade as industrialism develops, need not be shown at length.

Foregoing instances make it clear that they are still maintained vigorously in societies characterized by that type of organization which continuous war establishes; and that they prevailed to considerable degrees during the past warlike times of more civilized societies. Conversely, they show that as, along with the rise of a wealth which does not imply rank, luxuries and costly modes of life have spread to those who do not form part of the regulative organization; the growth of industrialism tends to abolish these marks of class-distinction which militancy originates. No matter what form they take, all these supplementary rules debarring the inferior from usages and appliances characterizing the superior, belong to a social *régime* based on coercive co-operation; while that unchecked liberty which, among ourselves, the classes regulated have to imitate the regulating classes in habits and expenditure, belongs to the *régime* of voluntary co-operation.

Source: from *The Principles of Sociology* (Williams & Norgate, London, 1893) pp. 49-54, 76-80, 113-34, 143-9, 152-4, 172-3, 194-204.

14 THE RULING CLASSES

Gaetano Mosca

The two traditional classifications of the forms of government are those of Aristotle and Montesquieu. The former distinguished between monarchies, aristocracies, and democracies, depending on whether sovereign power was vested in a single person, a restricted class, or in the totality of the citizens. Montesquieu defined as despotic those regimes in which the power of the sovereign was un-restrained by any custom, local or class privilege, or his own law; a monarchy, he said, was a state in which the ruler was subject to those restraints, and all organizations with non-hereditary heads of state he labeled as republics of the democratic or aristocratic type, depending on whether sovereignty belonged to all or only a part of the citizens.

These classifications have this common defect, that they are based on observation of a single moment in the evolution of political organisms. In the case of Aristotle, the model was the Greek polis of the fifth and fourth centuries B.C.; Montesquieu considered only the conditions which existed in the Europe of his time, when Venice, Genoa, and Switzerland did not have a heridatary chief of state, when France was governed by a monarchy which to a certain extent was limited by custom, a relatively independent judiciary, and by the privileges of the upper classes and the corporations, and Turkey was ruled by a unique despot who, apparently, did as he pleased. Between the lines, the author of *The Spirit of the Laws* let it be known that his ideal was the tempered monarchy as it existed at the time in England.

The other, more important, defect of the two traditional classifications is the superficiality of the criteria on which they are based. They take into account the formal rather than the really substantial differences between the various political organisms. Speaking of Montesquieu, it is not difficult to prove that there is more dissimilarity between the governments he calls republics than between some of them and certain monarchies. For instance, the United States has today surely less in common with the French Republic than the latter has with the Kingdom of Belgium; it is hardly necessary to mention the great differences between the republics of our time and those of medieval times or of antiquity. If we consider Aristotle's scheme, we see at once that it is quite impossible for one man to rule over millions of subjects without the assistance of a hierarchy of officials or a ruling class, and equally impossible for a democracy to function without a co-ordinating and directing body which again will be an organized minority, another ruling class.

Today, a whole new method of political analysis attempts to draw attention to that very fact; its major purpose is to study the formation and organization of that ruling stratum which in Italy is by now generally known by the name of *political class* — an expression which together with the term *elite,* used by Pareto, begins to find international acceptance.

To be exact, the method is not altogether new, for the importance of, and the need for, a ruling class had already been intuitively recognized in isolated instances in antiquity, and later by such men as Machiavelli, Guicciardini, and Rousseau. Even more authors had that intuition in the nineteenth century, foremost among whom was Saint Simon. But it was only toward the end of that century and afterwards that the new vision became diffused.

One of the first results of the new method was the notion of what, since 1883, has been known as the *political formula,* meaning that in all societies, be their level ever so mediocre, the ruling class will justify its power by appealing to some sentiment or credence generally accepted in that period and by that society, such as the presumed Popular or Divine Will, the notion of a distinct nationality or Chosen People, traditional loyalty toward a dynasty, or confidence on a man of exceptional qualities.

Of course, every political formula must reflect the specific intellectual and moral maturity of the people and the epoch in which it is adopted. It must closely correspond to the particular conception of the world prevailing at that time in that particular society, in order to cement the moral unity of all the individuals who compose it.

Any indication that a political formula has become 'dated', that the faith in its principles have become shaky, that the ardent sentiments which once inspired it have begun to cool down is a sign that serious transformations of the ruling class are imminent. The French revolution came when the great majority of Frenchmen ceased to believe in the divine right of kings, and the Russian revolution broke out when virtually the whole intelligentsia, and perhaps also the majority of the Russian workers and peasants, had stopped believing that the Tsar had received the right from God to govern Holy Russia autocratically.

Vice versa, when a political formula is in harmony with the mentality of the epoch and in tune with the prevailing sentiments of the nation, its utility is undeniable: it often serves as a check on the power of the ruler and ennobles somewhat the subjection of the ruled, making it appear less the result of merely brute coercion.

Given the fact that a ruling class is necessary to the functioning of all political organisms, it is evident that the study of political phenomena must focus upon the examination of the various ways in which the ruling class is formed and organized.

As concerns organisation, one may say that, up to now, three types existed: the feudal, the bureaucratic, and the third, less frequent but with an impressive intellectual heritage and quite important in its times, the Greek-Italian city-state.

The system which, in accord with the historical tradition, we call feudal is the simplest and most primitive of the three. It is also the least satisfactory because it rarely succeeds in co-ordinating all the ofrces of a people in pursuit of one and the same end, in peace or war. Its main characteristic is the fragmentation of the state into small parts, in each of which the representative of the supreme lord approximates to himself all sovereign powers. That is what happened in medieval Europe when the baron was at the same time the military chief and the chief civil magistrate and also had the right to levy taxes and all kinds of tributes in his fief.

The result was to make each part of the state so independent of the center that complete secession became relatively easy. Accordingly, the the unity of any feudal state and the cohesion between its component parts could be maintained only when the central organ was administered by a superior ruler of enough prestige and energy to overawe the local chieftain, or else when the national sentiment was sufficiently developed to hinder the dismemberment of the state, as was the case in Japan prior to the *Tokugawa Shoguns* early in the eighteenth century.

The bureaucratic system is characterized by the fact that the governmental functions are distributed not geographically but according to their nature. The military tasks thus become separated from the administrative-judicial duties, and these from financial operations. Each attribute of sovereignty is now entrusted to as many special hierarchies of officeholders, each of which receives its impulse from the central organ of the state. With the various activities of government distributed among different persons, the action of the small group which presides over the state becomes much more efficient and secure; conversely, there is little chance for any part to break away and achieve independence from the state.

The ancient oriental monarchies and the Mohammedan states usually retained a feudal character. In contrast, we can find in ancient Egypt traces of an evolution toward state bureaucracy. Bureaucratization can be likewise ascertained during the happier periods of Chinese civilization, although the provincial governors retained great power. Even greater was the independence of the Persian satraps, and there is no doubt that excessive local independence was one of the main causes of the relatively rapid, dissolution of the Caliphate of Baghdad and of the Moghul empire.

The transition from the feudal to the bureaucratic stage is usually quite slow. A typical example is the development of France, where the struggle between central monarchy and feudalism lasted almost seven centuries, from Hugh Capet to Louis XIV. Disintegration of a bureaucratic state is rarer than the dissolution of a feudal organism, but when it happens, as for instance in the case of the Western Roman Empire in the fifth century A.D., the collapse is likely to be more complete and more enduring than that of a feudal system, and the breakdown of the political machinery will be accompanied by a change of the moral forces and by the deterioration of the economic strength which that society had previously enjoyed.

We have already mentioned the characteristics that distinguished the old city-states of Greece and Rome from the other two types of government — characteristics which can only be discovered in the medieval communes rising throughout Western Europe after A.D. 1000. In these as in the old city-states the ruling class was, at least in appearance, very large, including (given the short tenure and the fast rotation of all public offices) a good-sized portion of the citizenry. In fact, however, the important offices were almost always controlled by the members of a certain number of illustrious families. That was particularly so in Rome; in Greece the democratic current triumphed in imposing absolute equality on all the citizens, but the accompanying civil wars, and the spoilation of the rich that went with them, prepared the ground for the formation of tight oligarchies, which in turn produced the tyrant.

In the medieval commune, too, the most important offices were as a rule reserved for the heads of the major craft guilds or, as in Venice, for a certain number of distinguished families. Where such a power concentration in a limited group did not occur, the commune almost invariably gave way to a *signoria,* the equivalent of the ancient tyranny.

It is a well known fact that hardly ever did the old polis or the medieval commune manage to extend its boundaries and at the same time keep intact the principles on which the state was based. Only the political wisdom of Rome could partly overcome that difficulty, but when her dominion had expanded to all corners of the Mediterranean, even Rome was finally forced to adopt a bureaucratic form of government.

Still, the strength and the resilience of the city-state in an emergency surpassed by far the limitations of its size. Thus Athens, after having lost all but a few of the forty thousand men sent on the ill-fated Sicilian expedition, remained strong enough to withstand the Peloponnesian League for almost another decade. Rome's immense losses did not prevent her from winning the first and second Punic wars, and Pisa, which in the thirteenth century never had more than eighty thousand inhabitants, suffered no less than five thousand casualties and eleven thousand prisoners in the battle of La Meloria alone. The Athenian, Florentine, Venetian contributions to the arts and sciences are too well known to require more than a brief mention.

The intellectual influence exerted by this form of government was, in conjunction with some other factors, favorable to the evolution of that type of social and political organization which may be called liberal, in distinction from that other type which may be labeled autocratic. The main characteristic of the liberal system consists in the fact that in it power is transmitted from the bottom to the top. That is, the functionaries are elected by the citizens who subsequently are expected to obey them, whereas in the autocratic system the supreme chief appoints his immediate aides who in turn appoint the lower officials.

The last-named system was in force in the old oriental monarchies, the Moslem states, the Roman and Byzantine empires and, with certain limitations, also in the Western European monarchies from the sixteenth to the early nineteenth century. As examples of the liberal regime we may list, in addition to the ancient city-states and medieval communes, the various republican governments and parliamentary monarchies, although they may as well be classified as a mixed type, since their bureaucracies, which control a good part of the effective power, are almost always recruited along autocratic lines.

In general, the autocratic regimes may be said to have a greater staying power than the liberal regimes. The organism of the latter is so delicate that it will function only under suitable conditions, preferably in periods of economic prosperity and of great intellectual flowering. It would be naive to assume that the regimes called liberal are actually based, as their political formula claims, on the explicit consent of the popular majority. As I have demonstrated elsewhere, the electoral contest takes place between organized minorities controlling the disorganized majority of voters, who may choose between a small number of candidates presented by those minorities.

Still, the necessity to make a bid for the allegiance of the vast, unorganized majority obliges each of those groups to adapt itself, if only in appearance, to the thoughts and sentiments prevailing among the masses. That necessity sometimes enables liberal regimes to display an amazing vigor, but it has also the effect of forcing the ruling class to play up to the great majority of people who are less aware of the true interests of the society. And that is why the greatest threat to liberal institutions comes from the extension of the suffrage to the most uncultured strata of the population.

Even more important than the examination of the various types of ruling class, is the ability to rule. It is, as Saint Simon already knew, the sum of all the personal characteristics most appropriate to the direction of a certain people in a certain period. Add to it the will to rule and the conviction of possessing the right qualities — qualities which undergo continuous change as the conditions of each people in intellectual, moral, economic, as well as in military matters change continuously, with the result that each people's political and administrative arrangements also need appropriate modifications.

These modifications may take place gradually, in which case the new elements who infiltrate the ruling class will not effect a radical change in its attitude and structure. If, on the contrary, the changes in the composition of the ruling class take place in a tumultuous and rapid fashion, the replacement of the old minority by the new elements may be almost completed in the course of one or two generations. In the first case, the prevailing influence is, as we called it elsewhere, the aristocratic tendency; in the second it is the one which we called the democratic.

It is rather difficult if not impossible to nullify completely either one of these two tendencies. The absolute predominance of the aristocratic tendency would presuppose that the ideas and conditions of human association never change; experience shows the absurdity of that assumption. On the other hand, the democratic tendency could absolutely triumph only on condition that the sons would not inherit the means, contacts, and advantages in training which enabled their progenitors to capture all the choice positions.

The private ownership of land and capital has been regarded as the major cause responsible for the hereditary nature of political control. Now I shall not deny the modicum of truth contained in that assertion. But we have already seen, to our satisfaction, that the state control of the means of production would leave the administrators of the state — who are sure to be a minority — in a position where they should be able to combine all economic and political power in their hands and to appropriate the largest share in such a manner as would advance the career of their own sons and proteges.

In the remote past, rapid and almost complete renewals of the ruling class took place not infrequently in the wake of an irruption of barbaric tribes which had not yet found a fixed habitat. They established themselves in the conquered country and supplanted there the previous rulers. Very often the success of the invaders was due to the discord and the decadence of the old dominant minority, and almost always to the apathy, sometimes to the connivance, of the lower class in the invaded territory.

These political cataclysms were not at all rare events in the oriental empires of antiquity. The Mesopotamian civilization suffered several of them, and the havoc which the Hyksos worked in Egypt is a well-known story. Invasions of the same type were, at various intervals, the ruin of the Chinese and Indian civilizations; the fall of Rome and the invasions of the Arabs and Turks are all part of the same chronicle.

With the progress of civilization, the zone populated by barbarians became more and more restricted, while the densely settled areas of industrious, peaceful agriculturers and artisans increased apace. A much improved technology put into their hands weapons of defense which had not been available against the raiders led by Ghengis Khan and Tamerlane. Catastrophes caused by external forces have thus become more and more unlikely, if not utterly impossible.

In our time, the violent convulsions of the social order are the product of internal factors. The ruling class, attacked by a political force from below, disintegrates. Instead of invasions, we have today revolutions. It will suffice to mention here the great French revolution; what took place in Japan between 1853 and 1866 may well be called a revolution too. And there is finally the Russian revolution, the most violent of all. But no matter how violent and whatever the causes of the cataclysms that revolutionize the composition and the structure of the ruling class, almost invariably some elements, more or less numerous, of the old ruling class will enter the ranks of the new.

From an objective study of historical events one may draw this conclusion: the best regimes, that is, those lasting a long time and able to avoid the violent convulsions which have plunged mankind back into barbarism, are the mixed regimes. We call them mixed because in them neither the autocratic nor the liberal principle rules supreme, and the aristocratic tendency is tempered by a gradual but continuous renewal of the ruling class, enabling it thus to absorb the better elements into its ranks. But in order that such a regime may long endure, conditions must exist which not even the wisest legislator can create by fiat. The necessary multiplicity and balance of the ruling forces, if they are to function well, require a highly civilized community. Also, the church ought to be separated from the state; economic decisions must not be monopolized by the political decision-makers; the means of violence must never be controlled by any single faction of the people; last, men of cultural and technical accomplishment ought to be given access to the ruling class.

But more is needed: a great deal of education, which is always a slow process, and long experience in devising the most practical means of domesticating the base instincts which so often are joint to the will to power — instincts which again and again reasserted themselves after a protracted period of political and social peace, just when they seemed to be extinct forever.

Source: from James H. Meisel, *The Myth of the Ruling Class : Gaetono Mosca and the Elite.* (Ann Arbor Paperbacks, University of Michigan Press, 1962) pp. 382-91.